TATE'S BAKE SHOP
COOKBOOK

ALSO BY KATHLEEN KING

✤

Kathleen's Bake Shop Cookbook

Kathleen King

TATE'S BAKE SHOP COOKBOOK

The Best Recipes from
Southampton's Favorite Bakery for
Home-Style Cookies, Cakes, Pies,
Muffins, and Breads

St. Martin's Press
New York

www.stmartins.com

Design by Kathryn Parise
Photographs by Alexandra Rowley

LIBRARY OF CONGRESS CATALOGING-IN-PUBLICATION DATA

King, Kathleen, 1958–
    Tate's Bake Shop cookbook / Kathleen King
        p. cm.
    ISBN 0-312-33417-6
    EAN 978-0-312-33417-8
    1. Baking I. Tate's Bake Shop. II. Title.

TX765.K52523 2005
641.8'15—dc22

                                        2004066063

First Edition: July 2005

10 9 8 7 6 5 4 3 2 1

For Zvi,

the sweetest thing in my life

I love you

Contents

POUND CAKES AND BREADS

19

COOKIES AND BARS

31

CAKES
101

HEALTHY ALTERNATIVES

141

Foreword

Everyone says, "I wish I had my own bakery or specialty food store." Sounds like fun, doesn't it? You hang out in the kitchen and test a fabulous chocolate cake. You travel to Milan to see what's new in food. Maybe you drop into the store on Saturdays to have a cup of coffee and chat with the customers. *Not exactly!*

Kathleen King opened Tate's Bake Shop in Southampton, New York, just a year or two after I opened Barefoot Contessa in nearby Westhampton Beach. I wish I could say that we spent a lot of time together in those early years, but, instead, we were each working twenty-hour days, seven days a week. I know it was as much fun for Kathleen as it was for me, but it was also an amazing amount of hard work. Kathleen is totally hands-on and she's a bundle of energy. When she decides to make lemon bars, she tests the recipe over and over again until it's *absolutely* perfect, and then she sees it all the way through large-scale production. Almost anyone can make twelve really good lemon bars. Kathleen knows how to make twelve thousand really good lemon bars—and, believe me, that's not easy.

As soon as Kathleen opened her doors in 1980, Barefoot Contessa carried everything she made: chocolate chip cookies, oatmeal cookies, lemon bread, carrot cakes, sour cream coffee cakes...even the most delicious doughnut holes. Every day we placed an enormous order and every night the shelves were empty.

These weren't just any chocolate chip cookies; they were the best chocolate chip cookies you ever ate. Over the past twenty-five years, Kathleen has developed an amazing line of baked goods—from moist blueberry muffins, to delicious raspberry squares, to her famous carrot cake with cream cheese icing. Sure, you could get in your car and drive all the way to Southampton to pick up a bag of goodies, but Kathleen has shared her secrets in this book, so now you can make all of her famous baked goods right at home. Start with the chocolate chip cookies.

—*Ina Garten*

Preface

When I was a little girl, growing up on North Sea Farms, in Southampton, Long Island, I dreamed of being a veterinarian. I loved playing and caring for all the animals, but by the time I reached high school, I realized that I didn't have the scientific mind to achieve that goal.

Growing up on a farm is a bit different from the norm. Hard work, independence, and common sense are taught at a very early age. I can still hear in my mind: "Work hard," "Use two hands," "Think," and "Just do it, because no one is going to do it for you!" Everyone on a farm is a team player, and you had better fulfill your responsibility. I have one sister and two brothers, but there were no boy jobs or girl jobs; there were just jobs!

I started baking cookies when I was eleven years old in order to buy my own school clothes. My mom would go and buy the ingredients at the store, and I would bake the cookies in our home kitchen. As time went on, Mom's kitchen became my playground, and my little cookie business began to grow and grow.

When I realized that being a veterinarian was not a practical goal for me, I began to focus more on my cookie business. Famous Amos was my idol. I used to fantasize that he would pull up in his big Cadillac and purple outfit to buy my cookies. Whenever a bake shop was written up in the *New York Times*, I would tell my brother, "One day that that will be me."

That day did come. I went into business in 1980 when I was twenty years old. Within the first year, I *was* written up in the *New York Times*! My success happened rather quickly, and I just baked and baked in order to keep up with the demand. It was all a bit shocking, but I kept at it, always trying to do my best and giving our customers the best products that we could. I added muffins, pies, brownies, and cakes to our already famous cookie line.

When I was twenty-three, I moved out of my rented building into the present home of Tate's Bake Shop. The building was made just for me. Lots of windows and light and a wonderful country atmosphere that makes a stop at Tate's Bake Shop so appealing.

After twenty-six years in the baking business, we still sell the same quality products that attract customers from all over. My staff takes pride in their work, and a lot of customers are now bringing their children into the bake shop. Having a bake shop all these years has not always been easy, but it has been rewarding and fulfilling. Being a part of Southampton has been a blessing.

Acknowledgments

I cannot thank anyone before expressing my extreme gratitude to the people of the Hamptons, those I know and those I don't, for always standing by me and supporting me through some very bizarre times. The love and power that they gave me is the only reason Tate's Bake Shop exists.

To my parents, Millie and Tate King, for the strength and pride you taught me in order to survive all of life's ups and downs; you gave me a foundation that won't crumble and a love that is everlasting.

To Michael Naimy, my guardian angel on earth, who protects and advises me.

To David Lazer, Ralph Rosella, David Fleischer, and Jim Ash for their hard work, brilliance, and heart. I will never forget you all.

To my retail staff—Lucy Camacho, Juana Espinosa, Malin Stewart, and Matt Dexter—for adding joy to the bake shop and spreading it to all who come into the store. Everyone tells me you are the best. It is true!

To my kitchen staff, who are reliable and consistent day after day and who take pride in all that they do.

To Liberto Vasquez for making our cakes beautiful.

To Fredis Guerra. There are no words to describe my gratitude to you; you are an amazing person, and I thank you.

To Lupe Camacho and Florencio Rojas for baking quality, consistent products

day after day, year after year, through thick and thin. You are every employer's dream.

To Rachele Borruso and Michel Dobbs for allowing me to enjoy my life and the beauty of every day. You both bring a sense of calm and a professionalism that empowers everyone around you.

To Kenny Patrick for distributing all of Tate's Cookies to our hundreds of locations and for always caring about quality and our company. Many, many thanks for all the things you do.

To Rena Zacharias for keeping us detailed and in order. Also, thanks for keeping me going on my bicycle so that I didn't find myself "wearing these recipes"!

To Carla Glasser and Elizabeth Beier for driving me crazy. If it weren't for you, this book would have never been completed. Thank you for making it happen.

To Marian Lizzi for her enthusiasm in getting this book started. I missed you!

TATE'S BAKE SHOP COOKBOOK

Basics

All the recipes in this book should take less time to make than it would to go to a store to buy a commercially prepared baked good. I will tell you just a few simple things so that you will have good results. There is nothing worse than taking the time and gathering the ingredients to make a recipe and then having it not turn out well. I can't guarantee that you will love every recipe, but I can guarantee that every recipe works. I have offered a variety of different choices to suit almost everyone's palate, and I personally have tested every recipe in a home kitchen, using standard ingredients and tools.

This book collects my favorite recipes from the bakery and beyond. Some of the best and most-requested recipes—including my chocolate chip cookies—are repeated from my first book, which is now out of print.

Flour makes a big difference to the outcome of your product. In testing the recipes for this book, I used Gold Medal all-purpose flour. (In fact, I used over fifty pounds of it developing the recipes for this book!)

Whenever I make cookies, I use a 2-tablespoon ice cream scoop, and I suggest you do the same. This will ensure the correct yield and bake time, and give you more uniform, professional-looking cookies.

I love baking with Silpat baking mats. They make cleanup much easier, and there is no added butter to the product. Silicon paper works just as well.

I

Always use an oven thermometer to make sure the temperature is accurate. I did not use my convection oven, which I love for baking, in developing these recipes because I realize that most of you may not have one. If you have one and want to use it, cut down the temperature by 25 degrees and bake for less time.

You will notice that I use salted butter. I know that unsalted butter is considered the "proper" thing for baking, but most of us only have salted butter in our refrigerators and I actually prefer it, so keep it simple. If you prefer unsalted butter, use it, but make a minor adjustment to the salt quantity. The recipes I recommend unsalted butter for should take *only* unsalted.

For almost all my cakes, I line the bottom of the pan with waxed paper. It is maddening to make a beautiful cake only to have it stick to the pan!

I also like lining the pans for bars and brownies with aluminum foil so that I can pull the whole thing out in one slab and cut it into nice even pieces when it is cool.

Always preheat the oven and wait for it to reach the correct temperature. *Don't rush this part.*

If you need eggs at room temperature, just cover them with hot tap water for a couple of minutes and the insides will warm up.

The microwave is a great tool for softening butter and melting chocolate.

To prebake pie and tart shells, you can use a bag of dried beans as weights— and use them over and over. Just cool the beans when you remove them from the shell and store them in a Ziploc bag. Expensive ceramic or metal pie weights are nice, but you can get the same results for 99 cents.

When using nuts, use them as they are, or toast them in a 350-degree oven on an ungreased cookie sheet for 10 minutes for added flavor.

If you don't have buttermilk, make your own by adding 1 tablespoon of white vinegar to one cup of whole milk. Let it sit for 5 minutes before using it.

I like to keep prepared, unbaked pie and tart shells in the freezer. Doing the same will save you, too, a lot of time when you have to get dinner done in a hurry!

I also like to make crumb topping and freeze it in Ziploc bags. Top your pie or tart with the frozen crumb topping and bake it as is; there is no need to thaw it.

When measuring sticky ingredients like molasses and honey, warm up your measuring cup by filling it with hot tap water and dumping it out. This makes the sticky ingredients slide out of the measuring cup.

Don't be afraid to make the recipes your own by adding or omitting nuts, raisins, chocolate, or different spices.

Unless otherwise indicated, all spices are ground.

For grating and zesting, I love the Microplane grater. It needs only a gentle touch. You'll be amazed at how incredible it is.

Feel free to substitute walnut or hazelnut oil for the vegetable oil in recipes.

I always use pure vanilla extract. It's expensive, but a little goes a long way.

Most of all, *have fun!* Don't take it seriously. If you screw up, don't worry about it—they're only cookies!

MUFFINS AND SCONES

Blueberry Muffins

These muffins are so buttery and moist that they make a perfect muffin base. You can add whatever fruit you desire to them.

Preheat the oven to 400 degrees. Grease twelve 3 × 1½-inch muffin cups.

In a large bowl, stir together the flour, baking powder, baking soda, sugar, and salt.

In a medium bowl, combine the melted butter, milk, and eggs. Whisk the mixture until it is combined.

Combine the butter mixture with the dry ingredients and mix it lightly until just moistened. Fold in the blueberries. Spoon the mixture evenly into the prepared muffin cups.

Bake them for 25 to 30 minutes or until a cake tester or a toothpick comes out clean when inserted in the center of one muffin.

3 cups all-purpose flour
4½ teaspoons baking powder
½ teaspoon baking soda
1¼ cups granulated sugar
½ teaspoon salt
1 cup salted butter, melted
1¼ cups milk
2 large eggs, lightly beaten
2 cups fresh or frozen blueberries

Yield: 12 muffins

Carrot Muffins

When testing this Tate's Bake Shop recipe for home use, I worked late at night and thought I would wait and taste them in the morning. My husband left early for work and took the whole batch with him. When I asked if there were any left for me to try, he said, "No, everyone ate three"! In my world, that means this one is a winner. Carrot muffins have the taste of carrot cake, but they are not as sweet and rich.

2 cups all-purpose flour
2 teaspoons baking soda
2 teaspoons cinnamon
1/4 teaspoon salt
3/4 cup sugar
3/4 cup vegetable oil
3 large eggs
2 cups carrots, grated
1/2 cup pecans
1/2 cup raisins
2 teaspoons vanilla
1 apple, peeled and cored,
    chopped (1 3/4 cups)

Yield: 10 muffins

Preheat the oven to 400 degrees. Grease ten 3 × 1½-inch muffin cups.

In a medium bowl, mix the flour, baking soda, cinnamon, and salt.

In a large bowl, combine the sugar, oil, and eggs. Mix until they are well combined. Stir in the carrots, pecans, vanilla, and apple. Fold in the flour mixture.

Spoon the mixture evenly into the prepared muffin cups. (I like to use an ice cream scoop.) The muffin cups should be filled to the top.

Bake them for 20 minutes or until a cake tester or toothpick inserted in the center of a muffin comes out clean.

Mincemeat Muffins

Making muffins is a wonderful way to use up leftover mincemeat from the holidays. Even people who claim they don't like mincemeat will love these hearty muffins, especially if you don't tell them there is mincemeat in the muffin!

Preheat the oven to 400 degrees. Grease twelve 3 × 1½-inch muffin cups.

In a large bowl, stir together the flours, sugar, baking powder, and salt. In another bowl, stir together the mincemeat, eggs, water, oil, and vanilla until they are blended. Make a well in the center of the dry ingredients, add the mincemeat mixture and walnuts, and stir them until just combined.

Spoon the batter into the prepared muffin cups. Bake them for 20 to 25 minutes or until a cake tester or toothpick inserted in the center of one muffin comes out clean.

Remove the muffins to a wire rack and cool 5 minutes before removing them from the cups. Finish cooling them on the rack.

1 cup whole wheat flour
1 cup all-purpose flour
¼ cup white sugar
1 tablespoon baking powder
½ teaspoon salt
1¼ cups prepared mincemeat (page 95)
1 egg yolk
2 whole large eggs, lightly beaten
⅓ cup water
½ cup vegetable oil
1 teaspoon vanilla
1 cup walnuts, chopped

Yield: 12 muffins

Mocha Pecan Muffins

A not too sweet, not too chocolaty muffin that adults and children both enjoy.

2 cups all-purpose flour

¾ cup whole wheat flour

1 cup firmly packed dark or
  light brown sugar

⅓ cup Dutch-processed
  cocoa powder

1 teaspoon baking soda

½ teaspoon baking powder

1 teaspoon salt

½ cup vegetable oil

¼ cup salted butter, melted

3 large eggs

1 cup plain yogurt, low fat or
  full fat

½ teaspoon espresso
  powder dissolved in ½ cup
  water (or substitute a half
  cup of morning coffee)

1 teaspoon vanilla

1 cup pecans, chopped

1 cup mini chocolate chips

Yield: 12 muffins

Preheat the oven to 375 degrees.

Spray a 12-cup 3 × 1½-inch muffin tin with pan spray.

In a large bowl, combine the flours, sugar, cocoa powder, baking soda, baking powder, and salt.

In another large bowl, combine the oil, butter, eggs, yogurt, coffee mixture, and vanilla.

Fold the wet ingredients into the dry ingredients.

Fold in the pecans and chocolate chips.

Spoon the batter evenly into the prepared muffin cups. The cups will be very full, but don't worry, they won't overflow. The batter will rise up nicely, and the finished product will look beautiful.

Bake them for 25 minutes or until a cake tester or toothpick inserted into the center of one muffin comes out clean.

Cool the muffins completely in the pan.

Orange Poppy Seed Muffins

A very light citrus muffin with a flavor that can be changed to lemon or tangerine.

Preheat the oven to 400 degrees. Grease nine 3 × 1½-inch muffin cups.

In a medium-size bowl, stir together the flour, baking powder, baking soda, and salt.

In a large bowl, cream the butter and sugar until the mixture is light and fluffy. Add the egg yolks one at a time, beating well after each addition. Beat in the orange rind and the vanilla.

Add the flour mixture and buttermilk alternately to the butter mixture, finishing with the flour mixture. Fold in the poppy seeds. Beat the egg whites to soft peaks and fold them into the flour mixture.

Spoon the batter into the prepared muffin cups, filling them to the top.

Bake them for 20 minutes or until a cake tester or toothpick inserted in the center of one muffin comes out clean.

1 ¼ cups all-purpose flour
1 ¼ teaspoons baking powder
½ teaspoon baking soda
¼ teaspoon salt
½ cup salted butter, softened to room temperature
¾ cup sugar
2 large eggs, separated
1 tablespoon freshly grated orange rind
1 teaspoon vanilla
½ cup buttermilk
2 tablespoons poppy seeds

Yield: 9 muffins

Banana Chocolate Chip Muffins

When my nephew Nate Driscoll spent the summer with me, he was a big banana freak. Whenever I saw the bananas on the counter getting spots, I would turn them into something delicious, like these very rich and moist muffins.

2 cups all-purpose flour
2 teaspoons baking powder
½ teaspoon baking soda
½ teaspoon salt
½ cup salted butter
½ cup firmly packed dark or
    light brown sugar
¼ cup sugar
1 teaspoon vanilla
2 large eggs
1 ½ cups smashed banana
    (the darker the skin, the
    better for baking)
½ cup sour cream
1 cup chocolate chips

2 tablespoons turbinado or
    raw sugar for topping
    (optional)

Yield: 12 muffins

Preheat the oven to 400 degrees. Grease twelve 3 × 1½-inch muffin cups.

Mix the flour, baking powder, baking soda, and salt. Set it aside.

Cream the butter and the sugars until they are light and fluffy. Add the vanilla and eggs and mix everything well. Mix in the bananas and sour cream. Fold in the flour mixture. Fold in the chocolate chips.

Spoon the mixture into the prepared muffin cups. The cups will be very full, but don't worry, they won't spread over. Sprinkle them with turbinado sugar if you have it, but the muffins are fine without it.

Bake them for 20 minutes or until a cake tester or toothpick inserted in the center of one muffin comes out clean.

Rhubarb Crumb Muffins

I love the sweet, tart taste of rhubarb. This muffin could be served as a small cake topped with whipped cream or ice cream. When rhubarb first appears, make these for breakfast for a spring morning treat.

Preheat the oven to 375 degrees. Grease twelve 3 × 1½-inch muffin cups.

TO MAKE THE CRUMB TOPPING: Mix the flour, sugar, and cinnamon. Mix in the butter with your fingers or a pastry blender until the mixture forms small crumbs. Set it aside. (This can be made the night before and stored in a Ziploc bag; you can even freeze it.)

TO MAKE THE BATTER: Mix the rhubarb and sugar in a small bowl and set it aside.

Mix the flour, baking powder, and salt in a small bowl and set it aside.

Beat the butter and sugar together until they are light and fluffy, about 2 minutes. Add the eggs and vanilla and beat them until they are fluffy, about 1 minute. Slowly mix in half of the flour mixture until it is incorporated, then half of the milk. Mix it and scrape down the sides of the bowl. Repeat.

Fold in the rhubarb mixture.

Divide the batter evenly into the prepared muffin cups. Distribute the crumbs evenly on top of each muffin.

Bake them for 20 minutes or until a cake tester or toothpick inserted into the center of one muffin comes out clean.

CRUMB TOPPING

¾ cup all-purpose flour
⅓ cup firmly packed dark or
   light brown sugar
½ teaspoon cinnamon
5 tablespoons salted butter

MUFFIN BATTER

2 cups fresh rhubarb, cut
   into ¼-inch pieces
¼ cup confectioners' sugar
1¼ cups all-purpose flour
1 teaspoon baking powder
½ teaspoon salt
½ cup salted butter
   softened to room
   temperature
½ cup sugar
2 large eggs
½ teaspoon vanilla
½ cup milk

Yield: 12 muffins

Double Berry Crumb Muffins

A great all-purpose crumb muffin that tastes best with the freshest of summer berries.
Make any substitutions to suit your taste.

CRUMB TOPPING

¼ cup firmly packed dark or
   light brown sugar
¼ cup all-purpose flour
½ cup pecans, chopped
2 tablespoons salted butter,
   melted
1 ½ teaspoons grated orange
   zest from one orange

MUFFIN BATTER

1 ½ cups all-purpose flour
½ cup sugar
2 teaspoons baking powder
½ teaspoon cinnamon
¼ teaspoon salt
½ cup milk
½ cup salted butter, melted
1 large egg
1 cup blackberries, cut them
   in half if they are large
1 cup raspberries

Yield: 12 muffins

Preheat the oven to 400 degrees. Grease twelve 3 × 1½-inch muffin cups.

TO MAKE THE TOPPING: In a small bowl, combine the sugar, flour, pecans, butter, and orange zest. Mix it together until it is crumbly. Set it aside.

TO MAKE THE BATTER: In a large bowl, combine the flour, sugar, baking powder, cinnamon, and salt. In a separate small bowl, combine the milk, butter, and egg.

Add the milk mixture to the dry ingredients and fold them in. Fold in the berries and spoon the batter equally into the prepared muffin cups.

Spoon the crumb mixture evenly on top of each muffin.

Bake them for 20 minutes or until a cake tester or toothpick inserted in the center of one muffin comes out clean and the top is golden brown.

Oatmeal Scones

When I was living in England in 1979, I used to love what they called wholemeal scones. I am not exactly sure how they were made; but this is as close as I can remember.

Preheat the oven to 375 degrees. Grease two cookie sheets or line them with Silpat.

In a large bowl, stir together the flours, oatmeal, baking powder, sugar, and salt. Using two knives or a pastry blender, cut in the butter and blend it until the mixture is crumbly and the size of peas. Add the chopped dates. Slowly pour in the half-and-half while mixing continuously. Beat it for 1 minute. The dough will be sticky. Turn it out onto a floured board and knead it gently.

Roll out the dough on a lightly floured board to a thickness of ¾ inch. (I actually prefer to just pat it down gently to the thickness I want because this dough is very soft.) Cut the dough with a 3-inch round cutter lightly dipped in flour. Place the scones on the prepared cookie sheets about 2 inches apart.

Make an egg wash by beating the egg and sugar together. Brush it lightly on the top of each scone.

Bake the scones for 20 minutes or until they are slightly golden in color.

1 cup all-purpose flour
1 cup whole wheat pastry flour
2 cups old-fashioned rolled oatmeal
2 tablespoons baking powder
½ cup firmly packed dark or light brown sugar
¼ teaspoon salt
½ cup salted butter, cut into pieces
1 cup dates, pitted and chopped
1 ¾ cups half-and-half

1 large egg
1 teaspoon sugar

Yield: 14 large scones

Scott's Drop Scones

My friend Scott Goldsmith loves weekends in the Hamptons and shopping at the bake shop, but he has his own favorite scone recipe. What makes this one so easy is that you don't have to roll the dough out. These scones are best served warm.

2 cups all-purpose flour
¼ cup sugar
1 tablespoon baking powder
¼ teaspoon salt
¾ cup dried currants
1 ¼ cups heavy cream
2 tablespoons salted butter, melted

Yield: 12 scones

Preheat the oven to 425 degrees.

In a large bowl, combine the flour, sugar, baking powder, and salt. Mix the ingredients well and add the currants, breaking them apart with your hands if any are stuck together.

Add the heavy cream and mix with a fork until they are just combined. The dough will be sticky. Dump it onto a lightly floured board and knead it 6 to 8 times with the heels of your hands. Tear pieces of the dough off and drop them onto an ungreased cookie sheet. Pat down the dough to about 1-inch thick.

Brush the tops with the melted butter.

Bake the scones for 15 minutes or until they just begin to brown lightly.

Ginger Scones

Ginger is one of my favorite spices, especially around Christmastime. These scones are very light and simple. Serve them with orange marmalade and butter for a special presentation.

Preheat the oven to 375 degrees. Lightly grease one cookie sheet or line them with Silpat.

In a food processor, combine the flour, sugar, baking powder, cinnamon, ground ginger, cloves, and salt.

Add the butter and process until the mixture resembles coarse meal. Add the crystallized ginger and pulse once or twice to combine the ingredients.

Mix the half-and-half, egg, and vanilla in a separate bowl.

Add it to the flour mixture and process it until the ingredients are just combined.

Turn the dough out onto a lightly floured surface. Roll it out to a 1-inch thickness and cut it to the desired size. (I like scones small, so I use a 2-inch round cutter.)

Place the scones 2 inches apart on the prepared cookie sheet. Brush them with an egg wash made by beating one egg with 1 tablespoon of water. Sprinkle them with turbinado sugar.

Bake them for 20 minutes or until they are golden brown around the edges. Serve them warm.

2 cups all-purpose flour
½ cup firmly packed dark or light brown sugar
1 tablespoon baking powder
1 teaspoon cinnamon
¾ teaspoon ground ginger
⅛ teaspoon cloves
⅛ teaspoon salt
6 tablespoons salted butter, chilled and cut into small pieces
¼ cup chopped crystallized ginger
¼ cup half-and-half
1 large egg
1 teaspoon vanilla

1 large egg
2 tablespoons turbinado sugar (for topping)

Yield: 13 two-inch scones

Apricot Ginger Scones

We sell tons of scones at Tate's Bake Shop. I learned to make these when I studied in England. Traditionally, they are made with raisins, but this one is my favorite combination.

&

4 cups all-purpose flour

2 tablespoons baking powder

½ teaspoon salt

½ cup sugar

½ cup cold salted butter, cut into 8 pieces

1 cup dried apricots, chopped (I always use California apricots, and for this recipe I prefer them glacé.)

½ cup crystallized ginger, chopped

1¾ cups half-and-half

1 large egg

1 teaspoon sugar

Yield: 14 large scones

Preheat the oven to 375 degrees. Grease two cookie sheets or line them with Silpat.

In a large bowl, stir together the flour, baking powder, salt, and sugar. Using a pastry blender or two knives, cut in the cold butter and blend the ingredients until the mixture is crumbly and about the size of peas. Add the apricots and ginger and toss. Slowly pour in the half-and-half while mixing continuously. Mix the ingredients vigorously with a wooden spoon for 1 minute, or use a mixer with a paddle attachment.

Roll the dough out on a lightly floured board to a thickness of ¾ inch. Cut it with a 3-inch round cutter lightly dipped in flour. Place the scones on the prepared cookie sheets about 2 inches apart.

Make an egg wash by beating the egg and sugar together. Brush the egg wash lightly on top of each scone.

Bake the scones for 25 to 30 minutes or until they are light golden in color.

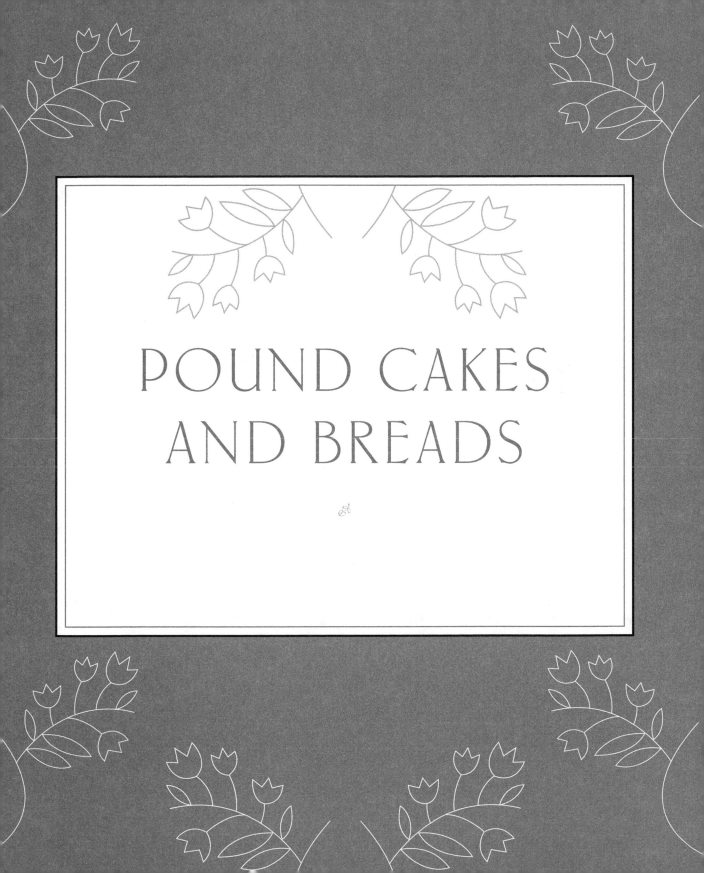

POUND CAKES
AND BREADS

Sour Cream Pound Cake

Nancy Hardy is a great home baker in Southampton. She shared a few of her recipes with me many years ago, and this pound cake was one of the winners—very moist, sweet, and flavorful. Serve it plain, with fruit and fresh cream, or drizzle it with your favorite lemon (recipe on page 24) or chocolate glaze (recipe on page 133).

⁂

Preheat the oven to 300 degrees. Spray a 10-inch Bundt pan with a nonstick spray.

In a small bowl, sift the flours, salt, and baking powder together. Set it aside.

Cream the butter and sugar with an electric mixer till it's light and fluffy.

Add the vanilla and mix it in.

Add the eggs one at a time, mixing and scraping down the bowl after each addition. Add the sour cream and mix it in.

Add the dry ingredients. Mix all till they are combined.

Spoon the mixture into the prepared pan.

Bake it for 1 hour and 30 minutes or until a cake tester or toothpick inserted in the center comes out clean.

NOTE: If you only have a 9-inch pan, bake the cake 15 minutes longer. It will rise over the top, but it will look very grand.

2½ cups all-purpose flour
½ cup cake flour
¼ teaspoon salt
½ teaspoon baking powder
1 cup unsalted butter, softened to room temperature
3 cups sugar
1 tablespoon vanilla
6 large eggs
1 cup sour cream

Yield: 1 ten-inch cake

Peanut Butter Bread

A wonderful moist tea loaf that tastes just like peanut butter. Eat it plain, toasted with your favorite jam, or go crazy and serve it with chocolate ice cream!

2 cups all-purpose flour
1 tablespoon baking powder
1/2 teaspoon salt
1/4 cup salted butter,
    softened to room
    temperature
1/2 cup sugar
1/4 cup firmly packed dark
    brown sugar
1 cup creamy peanut butter
1 large egg
1 teaspoon vanilla
1 cup milk

Yield: 1 nine-inch loaf

Preheat the oven to 350 degrees. Grease a 9 × 5 × 3-inch loaf pan and set it aside.

In a small bowl, combine the flour, baking powder, and salt. Set aside.

Cream the butter and sugars till they are combined. Add the peanut butter and mix it in. Add the egg and vanilla. Scrape down the sides of the bowl and mix again. Add the flour mixture. Blend until combined. The mixture will be dry. Slowly pour in the milk and mix well.

Spoon the batter into the prepared loaf pan.

Bake it for 50 minutes or until the center springs back when pressed with a fingertip.

Cool the loaf for 10 minutes in the pan and remove the bread from the pan to a cooling rack to cool completely.

Chocolate Pound Cake

This is one of my favorite pound cakes at Tate's. It is not as rich as a brownie and not as light as devil's food cake. This cake is perfect plain or even better with ice cream and raspberry sauce (recipe on page 113) or with fresh strawberries and whipped cream.

Preheat the oven to 325 degrees. Grease a 10-inch Bundt pan.

Sift the cocoa powder, flour, salt, and baking powder into a small bowl and set it aside.

Put the butter and sugar in a bowl. With an electric mixer, beat them till they are light and fluffy. Add the eggs one at a time, mixing well after each. Add the vanilla. Scrape down the sides of the bowl.

Mix the sour cream and water.

Add the dry ingredients alternately with half of the sour cream mixture in three stages, beginning and ending with the flour mixture and scraping down the sides of the bowl between stages.

Spread the batter into the prepared Bundt pan.

Bake it for 1 hour. Remove it from the oven and let it cool completely in the pan. Turn it out onto a wire rack to cool completely. This cake keeps very well and freezes well, too.

1 cup Dutch-processed
  cocoa powder
1 1/3 cups all-purpose flour
1/2 teaspoon salt
1/2 teaspoon baking powder
1 cup salted butter, softened
  to room temperature
2 cups sugar
4 large eggs
1 1/2 teaspoons vanilla
1/2 cup sour cream
3 tablespoons water

Yield: 1 ten-inch Bundt cake

Lemon Pound Cake

The lemon flavor really comes through in my lemon pound cake. It keeps well and freezes well, and is exceptional on its own or with fresh berries and cream.

❧

2¾ cups all-purpose flour
½ teaspoon baking soda
¾ teaspoon salt
1 cup unsalted butter,
　softened to room
　temperature
2½ cups sugar
1 teaspoon vanilla
1 tablespoon grated lemon
　zest
5 large eggs at room
　temperature
1 cup sour cream
½ cup fresh lemon juice,
　from about 4 lemons

LEMON GLAZE

½ cup fresh lemon juice,
　from about 4 lemons
½ cup sugar
¼ cup water

Yield: 1 ten-inch Bundt cake

Preheat the oven to 350 degrees. Prepare a 10-inch Bundt pan with lots of pan spray and sprinkle it with granulated sugar. (Flour will leave an unattractive residue on the cake.)

TO MAKE THE CAKE: In a medium bowl, combine the flour, baking soda, and salt. Set it aside.

In a large mixing bowl, cream the butter and sugar until they are light and fluffy. Add the vanilla and lemon zest. Mix them together. Add the eggs one at a time, mixing well after each addition. Scrape down the sides of the bowl.

Mix the sour cream and lemon juice together. Add the flour and sour cream mixture alternately, finishing with the flour. Spoon the batter into the prepared pan.

Bake it for 1 hour or until a cake tester or toothpick comes out clean when inserted in the center.

TO MAKE THE GLAZE: Mix all the ingredients in a small saucepan and stir. Cook them over low heat without stirring till the sugar dissolves. Turn the heat up to medium and cook the mixture until it becomes syrupy. Don't overcook it or the syrup will start to turn brown.

When the cake is baked, cool it for 10 minutes in the baking pan and invert it onto a plate. (Place the plate against the bottom of the pan and turn it over.)

Slowly pour the glaze over the cake and let it cool.

Corn Bread

This recipe makes a dense and moist loaf that is ideal for breakfast, toasted with butter, or served at dinner. You can make it less sweet by cutting down the sugar. If you want it a bit more savory, feel free to add jalapeños, green chilis, cheddar cheese, or whatever interests you. Corn bread is one of my most requested home recipes.

Preheat the oven to 350 degrees. Grease a 9 × 5 × 3-inch loaf pan.

Mix the flour, cornmeal, sugar, baking powder, baking soda, and salt in a medium bowl.

In a large bowl, whisk together the eggs, oil, milk, and sour cream. Fold in the dry ingredients until just incorporated. (If you are adding fresh corn, shuck it, cut the kernels from the cob with a sharp knife, then fold the kernels into the batter.)

Pour the mixture into the prepared pan and bake it for 15 minutes. Reduce the heat to 325 degrees and continue baking for 45 to 50 minutes, or until a cake tester or inserted toothpick comes out clean.

Cool the bread in the pan on a wire rack. Remove it after 5 minutes.

1 ½ cups all-purpose flour
1 ¼ cups yellow cornmeal
½ cup sugar
½ teaspoon baking powder
½ teaspoon baking soda
½ teaspoon salt
2 large eggs
½ cup vegetable oil
½ cup milk
½ cup sour cream
1 ½ cups fresh corn (about 2 ears) (optional)

Yield: 1 nine-inch loaf

Date Nut Bread

This date nut bread has lots of contrast and flavor. It is delicious on its own or as a base for ice cream. Try more interesting flavors like ginger, caramel, or pumpkin. Vanilla; of course, is always good. At breakfast, toast the slices and serve it with cream cheese; it's a nice change from a plain bagel or toast.

&

¾ cup boiling water
1 cup packed pitted dates, chopped small, about 6 ounces
1 ½ cups all-purpose flour
¼ cup instant quick oats
2 ¼ teaspoons baking powder
1 teaspoon cinnamon
¼ teaspoon salt
½ cup salted butter, softened to room temperature
¾ cup firmly packed dark brown sugar
1 large egg
1 egg yolk
2 tablespoons dark molasses
½ cup unsweetened applesauce
1 cup pecans, chopped
2 tablespoons crystallized ginger, finely chopped

Yield: 1 nine-inch loaf

Preheat the oven to 350 degrees. Grease one 9 × 5 × 3-inch loaf pan.

In a small bowl, combine the boiling water and chopped dates. Set them aside to soften.

In another large bowl, combine the flour, oatmeal, baking powder, cinnamon, and salt. Set it aside.

In a large bowl, cream the butter and sugar until they are well blended. Add the egg and egg yolk. Mix them well. Scrape down the sides of the bowl and mix again. Add the date mixture, molasses, and applesauce. Mix all the ingredients well.

Add the flour mixture to the date mixture and blend. Stir in the pecans and crystallized ginger.

Spoon the mixture into the prepared loaf pan. Bake it for 1 hour or until a toothpick or cake tester inserted in the center comes out clean.

Anadama Bread

When I was a kid my grandmother used to bring steaming hot loaves of this cornmeal-molasses bread to our home. The family would gather around our butcher-block table, cut off slabs of the bread, and spread them with butter and apricot jam. I had forgotten about this wonderful bread until my husband and I went to Maine last year and discovered a bakery in Bar Harbor that made it. Zvi fell in love with it, and we ate a loaf every day. Now I am baking it at home again!

Pour the boiling water into a large mixing bowl and stir in the cornmeal. Add the butter, molasses, and salt, and stir till all are combined. Cool the mixture to lukewarm.

Sprinkle the yeast into a half cup of warm water and stir it until it's dissolved. Add this to the cooled cornmeal mixture. Add enough flour to make a stiff dough and knead it on a lightly floured board until it is smooth and elastic.

Place the dough in a greased bowl and brush the top lightly with oil. Cover the bowl with plastic wrap and let the dough rise until it is doubled in bulk.

Punch down the dough and turn it out onto a lightly floured board. Divide the dough into two equal pieces. Shape each into a loaf and place them in a greased 9 × 5 × 3-inch pan. Brush each loaf with oil and cover the pans with plastic wrap.

Let the loaves rise again until doubled in bulk and bake them in a preheated 375-degree oven for 40 to 50 minutes or until the loaves sound hollow when tapped with your finger.

Remove the bread from the pans immediately and cool them on a wire rack.

2 cups boiling water
1/2 cup cornmeal
2 tablespoons salted butter
1/2 cup molasses
1 tablespoon salt
2 1/4-ounce packages instant dry yeast
1/2 cup warm water
7 to 8 cups all-purpose flour
1 tablespoon vegetable oil

Yield: 2 loaves

Zvi's Cinnamon Swirl Bread

My husband has been making this bread for years. Once when the outdoor temperature dropped to zero, we stayed in for the day and he taught me this recipe. It is fragrant when toasted, freezes beautifully, and makes an outrageous French toast.

CINNAMON BREAD

3 1/4-ounce packages active dry yeast

1/2 cup warm water (about 105 degrees)

1 1/2 cups warm milk

1/2 cup sugar (You can add more if you like it sweeter.)

1 tablespoon salt

1/2 cup salted butter

4 large eggs, lightly beaten, room temperature

8 cups all-purpose flour (You may use 3/4 cup more when kneading.)

SWIRL FILLING

1/2 cup salted butter, softened

3/4 cup firmly packed dark brown sugar

1 1/4 teaspoons cinnamon

Yield: three nine-inch loaves

TO MAKE THE BREAD: Dissolve the yeast in warm water in a large mixing bowl. If the bowl is cold, swirl hot water in it and empty it, so that the warm water doesn't cool down. Let it stand for 5 minutes.

Heat the milk, sugar, salt, and butter until warm to the touch. Do not boil.

Add the eggs, 4 cups of the flour, and the milk mixture to the yeast mixture. Mix with an electric mixer with a dough hook attachment, food processor, or stir by hand with a wooden spoon. Gradually add the remaining flour, mixing until it forms a stiff dough. This process will take about 10 minutes of mixing.

Remove the dough from the bowl, dust the board with flour, and knead the dough until it springs back when you press it with your finger and it is smooth and elastic. Place the dough in an oiled bowl three times the size of the dough. Roll it around once to coat it all over with oil. Cover it with a towel and let it rise till doubled in bulk, about 1 hour.

Grease three 9 × 5 × 3-inch loaf pans.

Punch down the dough and preheat the oven to 350 degrees.

TO MAKE THE FILLING: Cream the butter, sugar, and cinnamon. Set it aside.

TO FILL AND BAKE THE BREAD: Divide the dough into three equal portions, approximately 1½ pounds each. Roll out each piece into 8 × 12-inch rectangle.

Divide the filling evenly onto each rectangle and spread it over the entire surface, leaving a half-inch border. (I like to use my hands for this.) Sprinkle the filling with raisins and/or nuts if you like. (This is optional.) You can also double the filling if you like the filling gooey inside. Roll from the 8-inch side like a jellyroll. Pinch the edges and ends together. Tuck the ends under slightly and place the seam side down in the prepared pans.

Cover the bread with a towel and let it rise for another hour.

Bake the bread for 1 hour and 10 minutes.

Squash Rolls

My sister-in-law Robin King brings these rolls to our house every Thanksgiving. They have a beautiful orange color and are reminiscent of a soft white dinner roll.

1 1/4-ounce package active
  dry yeast
1/4 cup warm water
1/2 cup milk
1/2 cup cooked and mashed
  butternut squash
1/3 cup sugar
1 teaspoon salt
4 tablespoons salted butter
2 1/2 to 2 3/4 cups all-purpose
  flour

Yield: 12 rolls

Dissolve the yeast in 1/4 cup of warm water (about 105 degrees). Set it aside.

In a medium saucepan, scald the milk; then add the squash, sugar, salt, and butter. Remove it from the heat and add the yeast mixture.

In a large bowl, add the squash mixture to the flour and mix it well. On a lightly floured board, knead the dough till it is smooth and elastic. Put the dough in an oiled bowl, cover the bowl with plastic wrap, and let it rise until it's doubled in bulk.

Punch down the dough and turn it out onto a lightly floured board. Cut it into twelve equal portions and form it into rolls. Place the rolls side by side in a greased 9 × 13-inch pan. Cover them and let them rise until doubled in bulk.

Bake the rolls in a preheated 350-degree oven for 20 minutes or until they have a golden brown crust.

NOTE: Thawed frozen butternut squash or canned pumpkin can be substituted for the freshly mashed squash.

COOKIES
AND BARS

Cappuccino Shortbread

This basic cookie is thin and crisp, and is easy to put together when you need to make something quick for afternoon guests. You probably have most of these ingredients in your pantry. These cookies keep and freeze well.

Preheat the oven to 325 degrees.

Place all the ingredients except the chocolate in a medium mixing bowl. Mix the ingredients until they are combined. Add the chopped chocolate and mix till it's combined.

Put the mixture in an ungreased 9-inch square pan. Pat down the mixture evenly.

Bake them for about 30 minutes or until they are brown on the edges.

Remove the pan from the oven and cut the shortbread into desired sizes. Let it cool in the pan.

½ cup plus 2 tablespoons salted butter, softened to room temperature

1 ¼ cups all-purpose flour

2 teaspoons instant espresso powder

2 tablespoons firmly packed dark brown sugar

1 teaspoon cornstarch

½ cup confectioners' sugar

½ teaspoon vanilla

¼ teaspoon cinnamon

½ cup chopped semisweet chocolate

Yield: 32 small pieces or 16 large pieces

Polish Tea Cookies

Most of the customers at Tate's Bake Shop look for these Polish tea cookies as soon as the Christmas season arrives. The crisp buttery cookie surrounded by toasted nuts and filled with jam can make any holiday special. For fun, fill half of the cookies with green mint jelly and half with red raspberry jelly.

½ cup salted butter,
   softened to room
   temperature
½ cup sugar
1 large egg, separated
1 teaspoon vanilla
1 cup all-purpose flour
1 ½ cups chopped walnuts
Jelly or jam of choice

Yield: 27 cookies

Preheat the oven to 325 degrees. Grease two cookie sheets or line them with Silpat.

In a large bowl, cream the butter and sugar slightly. Add the egg yolk and vanilla and mix the ingredients well. Stir in the flour.

Roll the dough into small balls, the size of large marbles. Place the chopped walnuts on a piece of waxed paper. Dip the balls into the egg white and roll them in the chopped nuts. Place them on the prepared cookie sheets one and a half inches apart, and push down the center of each ball with your thumb.

Bake them for 5 minutes. Remove the cookie sheets from the oven, and press down the centers again using the back of a teaspoon. Bake them for 20 minutes more till they are golden brown.

While the cookies are still warm, fill them with your favorite jam or jelly. These cookies can be frozen just after rolling them in the nuts. To defrost them, just place the balls on cookie sheets until they are soft enough to press down the centers.

Ginger Hearts

Gingerbread hearts are soft, spicy, and chewy cutout cookies. The same dough can be used to make gingerbread men.

Preheat the oven to 350 degrees. Grease two cookie sheets or line them with Silpat.

In a large bowl, stir together the flour, baking powder, baking soda, salt, and spices.

In another large bowl, cream the egg and the sugar. Add the molasses and butter. Mix the ingredients well. Add all the dry ingredients and mix them until they are combined. Roll the dough into a ball, wrap it in clear film, and chill it for a half hour to one hour.

Roll the dough ¼-inch thick on a lightly floured board and cut it with a 2-inch heart-shaped cookie cutter that has been dipped in flour. Place the hearts 1½ inches apart on the prepared cookie sheets.

Bake the cookies for 10 minutes or until they are slightly firm to the touch. (Do not let the edges brown.) Don't overbake them or the cookies will be very hard. Remove them to a wire rack and cool.

2½ cups all-purpose flour
1 tablespoon baking powder
¼ teaspoon baking soda
½ teaspoon salt
¼ teaspoon allspice
1 tablespoon cinnamon
1 teaspoon ginger
1 teaspoon cloves
1 large egg
1 cup firmly packed dark
   brown sugar
⅔ cup dark molasses
½ cup salted butter,
   softened to room
   temperature

Yield: 52 two-inch hearts

Chocolate Chip Cookies

Chocolate chip cookies are our signature item. They are thin and crisp and remain every-one's favorite. Tate's Bake Shop bakes and sells thousands a week and ships them all over the country.

2 cups all-purpose flour
1 teaspoon baking soda
1 teaspoon salt
1 cup salted butter
¾ cup sugar
¾ cup firmly packed dark
    brown sugar
1 teaspoon water
1 teaspoon vanilla
2 large eggs
2 cups semisweet chocolate
    chips

Yield: 4½ dozen three-inch cookies.

Preheat the oven to 350 degrees. Grease two cookie sheets or line them with Silpat.

In a large bowl, stir together the flour, baking soda, and salt.

In another large bowl, cream the butter and sugars. Add the water and vanilla. Mix the ingredients until they are just combined. Add the eggs and mix them lightly. Stir in the flour mixture. Fold in the chocolate chips. Don't overmix the dough.

Drop the cookies 2 inches apart onto the prepared cookie sheets using two tablespoons or an ice cream scoop.

Bake them for 12 minutes or until the edges and centers are brown. Remove the cookies to a wire rack to cool.

Fruited Biscotti

This cookie is not too sweet—it's great after a heavy meal and not too rich for an afternoon tea. They are also nice for breakfast.

Preheat the oven to 350 degrees. Grease two cookie sheets or line them with Silpat.

Using an electric mixer, beat the eggs and sugar in a bowl until they are combined. Add the honey, oil, flour, baking powder, salt, and cinnamon. Mix them till they are just combined.

Stir in the almonds, pecans, apricots, dates, and sesame seeds.

Turn the dough out onto a floured board and divide the mixture in half. Roll each piece into a log about 14 inches long and 2 inches wide. Place the logs on the prepared cookie sheets, leaving 3 inches between them.

Bake them for 20 minutes. Remove the sheet from the oven and let the logs cool for 30 minutes on the sheet. Using a serrated knife, slice each log into ½-inch slices and place the slices on the cookie sheets cut side up. Bake them for 15 to 20 minutes more or until they are golden brown.

3 large eggs
½ cup sugar
¼ cup honey
½ cup vegetable oil
3 cups all-purpose flour
2 teaspoons baking powder
½ teaspoon salt
½ teaspoon cinnamon
½ cup whole almonds, chopped
½ cup pecans, chopped
½ cup dried apricots, chopped
½ cup dates, pitted and chopped
1 tablespoon sesame seeds

Yield: 48 cookies

37

Chocolate Biscotti

These biscotti are not too sweet or too chocolatey. They are not too hard, but are more light and crisp. My editor suggests serving them with Sambucca for a sophisticated dessert, but a simple cup of coffee on the side is more my style.

⌘

½ cup salted butter,
  softened to room
  temperature

⅓ cup firmly packed dark
  brown sugar

⅓ cup sugar

¼ cup unsweetened Dutch-
  processed cocoa powder

2 large eggs

1 ¾ cups all-purpose flour

2 teaspoons baking powder

¾ cup chopped milk
  chocolate

¾ cup chopped bittersweet
  chocolate

½ cup almonds, chopped
  small, blanched or
  unblanched

Yield: 40 biscotti

Preheat the oven to 375 degrees. Grease two cookie sheets or line them with Silpat.

In a large mixing bowl, cream the butter and sugars till the mixture is light and fluffy. Add the cocoa powder and beat it in for 2 more minutes. Beat in the eggs one at a time, scraping down the sides of the bowl after each addition. Stir in the flour and baking powder until they are just combined. Stir in the chocolates and almonds.

Chill the dough for 30 minutes.

Divide the dough into two equal parts and roll each piece into a 10-inch-long log. Place the logs on the prepared cookie sheets and flatten them to 1-inch thick by pressing them gently with your fingertips.

Bake them for 25 minutes. Then cool them for one hour on the cookie sheet.

Preheat the oven to 325 degrees.

Cut each log into ½-inch-wide diagonal slices. Place the slices on an ungreased cookie sheet, cut side up, and bake them for 10 minutes. Turn the cookies over and bake them for another 10 minutes. Cool them on the cookie sheets.

Old-Fashioned Soft Sugar Cookies

A professor at SUNY Cobleskill gave me this basic recipe while I was a student there. The cookies are a wonderful accompaniment to a fruit salad. You can also drizzle them with melted chocolate. I like them best in their simple state.

Preheat the oven to 350 degrees. Grease two cookie sheets or line them with Silpat.

In a medium bowl, combine the flour, baking soda, baking powder, and salt.

In a large bowl, cream the butter and sugar till the mixture is light and fluffy. Add the vanilla and egg. Mix it, scrape down the sides of the bowl, and mix it again. Add the sour cream and mix it till it is combined.

Add the flour mixture and mix it until it is combined.

Drop the cookies onto the prepared cookie sheets 3 inches apart. (They do spread.)

Bake the cookies for 15 minutes or until they are light brown. Cool them on the cookie sheets for 5 minutes, and remove them to wire cooling racks to cool completely.

3 1/4 cups all-purpose flour

1 teaspoon baking soda

1 teaspoon baking powder

1/4 teaspoon salt

3/4 cup salted butter, room temperature

2 cups sugar

1 tablespoon vanilla

1 large egg

1 cup sour cream

Yield: 44 cookies

Persimmon Cookies

These persimmon cookies are more like little round cakes than traditional cookies. They are spicy and cakey with all the pleasures of autumn. They don't spread, and if you use a little ice cream scoop to place them on a cookie sheet, they stay perfectly plump and round. One customer said, "They taste like Christmas!"

ॐ

1 1/4 cups Hachiya persimmon pulp (about 2 or 3 persimmons)

1/2 cup unsalted butter, softened to room temperature

1/2 cup sugar

1/4 cup firmly packed dark brown sugar

1 teaspoon grated orange rind

1 large egg

1 teaspoon vanilla

2 cups all-purpose flour

1 teaspoon baking soda

1/4 teaspoon salt

1 teaspoon cinnamon

1/2 teaspoon nutmeg

1/2 teaspoon cloves

1 cup walnuts, chopped fine

1/2 cup dried cranberries

Yield: 34 cookies

Preheat the oven to 350 degrees. Grease two cookie sheets or line them with Silpat.

For the persimmon purée, remove the stems from the persimmons and cut the fruit into chunks. Purée the chunks in a food processor till they are smooth.

Cream the butter and sugars till creamy. Add the orange rind, egg, vanilla, and persimmon pulp, and mix it. Add the flour, baking soda, salt, cinnamon, nutmeg, and cloves. Mix it all together. Add the walnuts and cranberries. Scrape down the sides of the bowl and mix it together until it is combined.

Drop the dough, using an ice cream scoop or two tablespoons, onto the prepared cookie sheets.

Bake them for 20 to 25 minutes, depending on the size. The cookies will spring back slightly when they are done.

NOTE: Persimmons should be very soft. They almost feel like they are overripe when they are ready. You can purée the persimmons and freeze or refrigerate the pulp for a few days.

Flourless Peanut Butter Chocolate Chunk Cookies

This cookie does not sacrifice flavor or texture even though it contains neither flour nor butter. All your friends will enjoy them, and the wheat-sensitive will love you!

Preheat the oven to 350 degrees. Grease two cookie sheets or line them with Silpat.

In a large bowl, mix the peanut butter, sugar, egg, baking soda, and vanilla extract until it is smooth and creamy. Stir in the chocolate.

To form each cookie into a ball, I use a small ice cream scoop, but you can also use your moistened hands. Place the dough on two ungreased cookie sheets; they don't spread a lot.

Bake the cookies 12 to 15 minutes, depending on the size you made, or until they are puffed and golden on the bottom. They will still be soft in the center. Cool them on the cookie sheets for a few minutes and then transfer them to a rack until they are completely cool.

1 1/4 cups peanut butter, smooth or chunky
3/4 cup firmly packed light brown sugar
1 large egg
1 teaspoon baking soda
1/2 teaspoon vanilla extract
1 cup semisweet minichocolate chips, or 1 bittersweet bar chopped fine

Yield: 40 one and a half-inch cookies, or 20 three-inch cookies.

Chuckies

For over a year my friend Chuck Forthofer requested that I make these cookies for him. Finally, on his birthday, I surprised him with one of his favorite treats. These cookies are chewier than my standard, but still thin. If you prefer a cakey cookie, increase the flour by a quarter cup.

2¼ cups all-purpose flour

1 teaspoon baking soda

¾ teaspoon salt

1 cup salted butter, softened to room temperature

1 cup firmly packed dark or light brown sugar

1 cup sugar

2 tablespoons corn syrup

2 teaspoons vanilla

2 large eggs

1½ cup bittersweet chocolate chunks

1½ cup macadamia nuts, toasted lightly and chopped

2 cups coconut, lightly toasted

Yield: 48 three-inch cookies

Preheat the oven to 350 degrees. Grease two cookie sheets or line them with Silpat.

TO TOAST THE MACADAMIA NUTS: Spread the nuts on an ungreased cookie sheet and bake at 350 degrees for 10 minutes, shaking the pan from time to time to turn the nuts over.

TO MAKE THE COOKIES: In a large bowl, stir together the flour, baking soda, and salt.

In another bowl, cream together the butter and the sugars. Add the corn syrup and vanilla. Mix them until they are just combined. Add the eggs and mix them lightly. Stir in the flour mixture and blend until just combined. Stir in the chocolate chunks, macadamia nuts, and coconut.

Using two tablespoons or a small ice cream scoop drop the dough onto prepared cookie sheets. These cookies will spread, so place them at least 2 inches apart.

Bake them for 18 minutes or until the edges start to brown and the centers are not too wet.

Cool them on the cookie sheets for 10 minutes and remove them to a wire rack to cool completely.

Double Peanut Chocolate Cookies

This very sweet, soft, and moist cookie contains peanut butter chips and chocolate chips. Kids love them.

❧

Preheat the oven to 350 degrees. Grease three cookie sheets or line them with Silpat.

In a small bowl, combine the flour, cocoa powder, and baking soda. Set it aside.

In a large bowl, using an electric mixer, combine the butter, sugar, and peanut butter till creamy. Add the vanilla. Add the eggs one at a time and mix well after each addition. Scrape down the sides of the bowl and mix again. Add the flour mixture and mix. Stir in the chips.

Using two tablespoons or a small ice cream scoop, drop the dough onto the cookie sheets. Space the dough so there are twelve cookies per tray.

Bake them for 12 to 15 minutes.

1 cup all-purpose flour

1/2 cup unsweetened cocoa powder

1/2 teaspoon baking soda

3/4 cup salted butter, softened to room temperature

1 cup lightly packed dark or light brown sugar

1/2 cup peanut butter, creamy or crunchy

1 teaspoon vanilla

2 large eggs

1 cup peanut butter chips

1 cup chocolate chips

Yield: 36 two- to three-inch cookies

Italian Sesame Seed Cookies

I am not a big fan of Italian cookies, but I have always loved the simplicity and texture of the standard sesame cookies that one finds in most pizzerias and bake shops. These cookies come so close that I no longer have to buy them!

&

½ cup salted butter,
   softened to room
   temperature
⅓ cup sugar
1 teaspoon vanilla
1 large egg
1 ¾ cups all-purpose flour
1 teaspoon baking powder
½ cup raw sesame seeds

Yield: 32 cookies

Preheat the oven to 375 degrees. Grease one cookie sheet or line it with Silpat.

Cream the butter and sugar till soft and creamy. Add the vanilla and egg. Mix them well.

Mix in the flour and baking powder.

Place the sesame seeds in a small bowl and set it aside.

Form the dough into small balls and roll them until they are smooth. Toss the balls one at a time into the sesame seeds, pressing lightly on all sides. Place them on the cookie sheet. I like to press gently so that I have a 2-inch long, 1¼-inch-wide cookie; these are about half the size of the commercial product. The cookies don't spread, so they can be placed fairly close together.

Bake them for 25 to 30 minutes or until they are golden brown all over.

Cool them on the cookie sheet.

Chocolate Chip Cookies (page 36)

Nancy Hardy's Pecan Pie (page 74)

Sour Cherry Pie (page 94)

Zvi's Cinnamon Swirl Bread (page 28)

Sour Cream Coffee Cake (page 128)

Double Berry Crumb Muffins (page 14)

Coconut Birthday Cake (page 138)

Chocolate Fudge Cupcakes (page 117) with Peanut Butter Icing (page 118)

Double Chocolate Almond Cookies

Nothing is better with a tall glass of milk or a cup of hot cocoa than this very soft, gooey, rich, chocolaty cookie.

Preheat the oven to 350 degrees. Grease two cookie sheets or line them with Silpat.

In a medium bowl, combine the flour, cocoa powder, baking soda, and salt.

In a large bowl, using an electric mixer, cream together the butter and sugars. Add the egg and vanilla and mix them together. Add the flour mixture and mix it till it's just combined.

Add the chocolates and almonds. Mix them till they are combined.

Using two tablespoons or a small ice cream scoop, drop the dough two inches apart on the cookie sheets.

Bake them for 15 minutes.

Cool the cookies on the cookie sheets. The cookies should be very soft when they are removed from the oven. They will firm up as they cool.

2 1/3 cups all-purpose flour
3/4 cup Dutch-processed cocoa powder
1 teaspoon baking soda
3/4 teaspoon salt
1 1/4 cups salted butter softened to room temperature
1 cup sugar
1 cup firmly packed dark or light brown sugar
1 large egg
1 teaspoon vanilla
1 cup white chocolate chips
1 1/2 cups semisweet chocolate chips
1 cup almonds, chopped

Yield: 52 cookies

45

Orange and Oat Chewies

One of my professors at SUNY Cobleskill College, Robert Sielaff, gave me this recipe. Robert's sister, Maryann Goschka, created and used it to win a Pillsbury bake-off contest. The simple flavors make a very chewy and sweet cookie.

2 cups all-purpose flour
1 teaspoon baking soda
½ teaspoon salt
2 cups rolled oats
2 cups firmly packed dark or light brown sugar
½ cup salted butter, softened to room temperature
½ cup Crisco
3 tablespoons frozen orange juice concentrate, thawed
Grated zest of one orange
2 large eggs
1 cup walnuts, chopped
⅓ cup shredded sweetened coconut

Yield: 42 cookies

Preheat the oven to 350 degrees. Grease two cookie sheets or line them with Silpat.

In a medium bowl, combine the flour, baking soda, salt, and oats.

In a large bowl, combine the sugar, butter, Crisco, orange juice, orange zest, and eggs. Mix them well. Add the flour mixture and blend. Add the walnuts and coconut and mix them till they are combined.

Drop the dough onto the cookie sheets using two tablespoons or a small ice cream scoop.

Bake them for 12 minutes until the edges become golden brown.

Cool them on the cookie sheets because the cookies are soft.

Nutella Shortbread
Sandwich Cookies

Cici, whom I met on a Costa Rican yoga retreat, had a passion for Nutella, a chocolate-and-hazelnut spread. When she invited our yoga group to a special fondue dinner, I made these cookies just for her.

Preheat the oven to 350 degrees. Grease two sheet pans or line them with Silpat.

Toast and skin the hazelnuts. In a food processor, pulse the hazelnuts with the sugar until they are finely ground. Add the flour and pulse again. Add the chopped butter and process it till the mixture comes together. Turn it out onto a work surface.

Roll it out to approximately ⅛-inch thickness. With any shape cookie cutter—I have used leaves, hearts, and circles—cut out the shapes and transfer the cookies to the prepared sheet pans.

Bake the cutouts for about 15 minutes, depending on their size and thickness. Cool the cookies on the sheet pans.

Spread the Nutella on one cookie and make a sandwich by topping the Nutella with another cookie.

½ cup hazelnuts
½ cup granulated sugar
1 ½ cups all-purpose flour
¾ cup cold salted butter,
   chopped into small pieces
½ jar of Nutella
   (13-ounce jar)

Yield: 16 two-inch sandwich cookies

Toffee Pecan Cookies

I love Heath Bars and I was so happy when their toffee bits appeared on the market. They can be found in the baking section of the supermarket near the chocolate chips. I was going to add chocolate to this recipe, but I thought that pecans would keep the flavor more intense. They can be made soft and chewy or crunchy. I prefer the crunchy, as did all my cookie fans at our local Scott J Aveda Salon.

1 ½ cups all-purpose flour
1 teaspoon baking soda
1 ½ cups instant quick oats
1 cup salted butter, softened
   to room temperature
1 cup firmly packed dark
   brown sugar
¼ cup white sugar
1 large egg
2 teaspoons vanilla
2 cups toffee bits

Yield: 42 cookies

Preheat the oven to 350 degrees. Grease two cookie sheets or line them with Silpat.

In a large bowl, combine the flour, baking soda, and oatmeal. Set it aside.

In another large bowl, cream the butter and sugars till creamy. Add the egg and mix well. Add the vanilla and mix. Scrape down the sides of the bowl and mix again.

Add the flour mixture to the butter mixture and beat them till they are combined. Don't overmix. Stir in the toffee bits and pecans.

Using two tablespoons, drop the cookie dough two inches apart onto prepared cookie sheets.

Bake them for 12 to 15 minutes for chewy cookies and 18 to 20 minutes for crunchy cookies. The crunchy cookies will be browner in the middle and firmer to the touch.

Double Chocolate Mint Cookies

My favorite chocolate combination is dark chocolate and mint. These cookies are soft and cakey with a hint of mint from the Andes Candies.

Preheat the oven to 375 degrees. Grease two cookie sheets or line them with Silpat.

Melt 1½ cups semisweet chocolate in a microwave or in a double boiler. Stir until just melted. Set aside and cool to room temperature.

In a small bowl, combine the flour, baking soda, and salt. Set it aside.

In a large mixing bowl, combine the butter, sugars, and vanilla. Beat them together until they are creamy. Add the eggs, scrape down the sides of the bowl, and mix again. Add the melted chocolate and beat the ingredients till they are light and fluffy.

Add the flour mixture and mix till it's just combined. Add the Andes Candies and the chocolate chips. Stir them until they are combined.

Drop the mixture by rounded tablespoonfuls or with a small ice cream scoop onto the prepared cookie sheets.

Bake the cookies for 10 minutes or until they spread and the centers don't look wet.

Let them stand for 2 to 3 minutes on the cookie sheets before removing them because the centers are very gooey when hot.

1 ½ cups semisweet
    chocolate chips
2 ½ cups all-purpose flour
1 ½ teaspoons baking soda
¾ teaspoon salt
1 cup salted butter, softened
    to room temperature
⅔ cup sugar
⅓ cup firmly packed dark
    brown sugar
2 teaspoons vanilla
2 large eggs
1 4.7-ounce box of Andes
    Crème de Menthe Candies,
    unwrapped and each piece
    broken in half
1 cup semisweet chocolate
    chips

Yield: 48 cookies

Chocolate Jumbles

Chocolate Jumbles are very sweet and cakey cookies. When we stopped making them at Tate's Bake Shop, customers were up in arms and ordered large batches to be shipped as far away as Florida. When my friend, Jill Zenker, was due to give birth to twin boys, I had to make an emergency delivery into Manhattan to satisfy her Jumble craving!

2½ cups all-purpose flour

½ cup Dutch-processed
cocoa powder

1 tablespoon baking powder

½ teaspoon salt

1 cup salted butter, softened
to room temperature

1½ cups firmly packed dark
or light brown sugar

2 large eggs

1½ teaspoons vanilla

2 cups white chocolate chips
or chunks

1 cup pecans, chopped

*Yield: Eighteen 3-inch
cookies*

Preheat the oven to 350 degrees. Grease two cookie sheets, or line them with Silpat.

In a large bowl, combine the flour, cocoa powder, baking powder, and salt. Set it aside.

Cream the butter and the sugar in a large mixing bowl. Add the eggs and vanilla. Mix and scrape down the sides of the bowl. Add the flour mixture and mix till it's just combined. Add the white chocolate chips and pecans. If the dough is too stiff, wet your hands and finish the mixing by hand. (Don't worry, it's not a big sticky mess.)

Using two tablespoons, drop the cookie dough onto the cookie sheets. Use an ice cream scoop if you have one. Wet it with warm water between scoops so the dough falls out easily. Press the dough balls down gently with your fingertips.

Bake the Jumbles for 20 minutes. The cookies will be soft when they come out of the oven. Do not overbake them.

Cool them on the cookie sheets for 5 minutes and remove the cookies to a wire rack to finish cooling.

Simple Lemon Wafers

These cookies are a little cakelike and have a fresh tang of lemon. These are delightful served with tea or fruit compote.

⁂

Preheat the oven to 350 degrees. Grease two cookie sheets or line them with Silpat.

Beat the butter and sugar with an electric mixer until light and fluffy. Beat in the egg until it is combined. Add the vanilla. Add the lemon juice and lemon zest.

Stir in the flour and salt. Mix them until they are just combined.

Drop teaspoonfuls of dough 2 inches apart onto the cookie sheet.

Bake the cookies for 8 minutes or until the edges are light brown.

Cool them for 2 to 3 minutes on the baking sheets and remove them to a wire rack to finish cooling.

1 cup unsalted butter, softened to room temperature
1 cup sugar
1 large egg
1 teaspoon vanilla
Grated zest and juice of 1 lemon
2 cups cake flour (not self-rising)
1/2 teaspoon salt

Yield: 48 cookies

My Favorite Cutout Cookies

I find the typical holiday cutout cookie is usually tasteless and hard. This one is light and crisp, buttery and delicious. If you want to decorate cookies with the kids, choose another recipe; this cookie is too fragile to be handled that much.

1 cup salted butter, cold
½ cup firmly packed dark or light brown sugar
2 teaspoons vanilla
1 ½ cups all-purpose flour
2 tablespoons cornstarch

Yield: 28 medium-size cutout cookies

In a food processor, combine the butter, sugar, and vanilla; process them until they are just combined.

Add the flour and cornstarch. Process the mixture until the dough comes together in a ball.

Form the dough into a flat disk, wrap it in clear film, and refrigerate it for at least one hour or overnight.

Preheat the oven to 350 degrees. Grease two cookie sheets or line them with Silpat.

Roll out the dough on a lightly floured surface until it is about ¼-inch thick; you can make them thinner if you wish, but not too much.

Cut the dough into desired shapes. Reroll the trimmings of the dough, roll it out, and cut it into more shapes until the dough has been used up. Place the cookies on prepared cookie sheets. These cookies don't really spread, so ½ inch apart will be fine.

Bake them for 10 to 15 minutes (depending on the size and thickness) until they are golden brown.

Gorp Cookies

I made this cookie with the intention of turning trail mix into a cookie. When I brought them to my friend Michael Marin, he immediately dubbed them Gorp Cookies and insisted I send them to all the summer camps in the country! They are thick and chewy and should give you enough energy to hike up the next mountain!

Preheat the oven to 350 degrees. Grease two cookie sheets or line them with Silpat.

In a small bowl, mix the flour, salt, and baking soda.

In a large mixing bowl, cream the butter and sugars. Beat in the egg.

Add the vanilla and water. Mix together until they are just combined.

Add the flour mixture and oatmeal. Mix them until they are combined.

Add the chocolate chips, peanuts, and raisins. Mix them until they are combined.

Drop ¼ cup of the cookies, 3 inches apart, onto the prepared baking sheets. Press the cookies down lightly.

Bake the cookies for 15 to 17 minutes. Remove the cookies and cool them on a wire rack.

½ cup all-purpose flour
¾ teaspoons salt
½ teaspoon baking soda
½ cup unsalted butter, softened to room temperature
½ cup firmly packed dark or light brown sugar
¼ cup sugar
1 large egg
1 teaspoon vanilla
1 teaspoon water
1 ½ cups rolled oats
1 cup semisweet chocolate chips
½ cup roasted peanuts
½ cup raisins

Yield: 14 large cookies

Chocolate Mint Brownies

I was served chocolate mint brownies one night at the home of my friend David Loewenguth.' His mother was visiting and baked his childhood favorite for him. I tried to copy it and had great success. These brownies taste like homemade Andes Candies.

&

BROWNIES

¾ cup all-purpose flour

¼ teaspoon baking soda

¼ teaspoon salt

2 cups semisweet chocolate chips

1 teaspoon vanilla

⅓ cup salted butter

⅔ cup granulated sugar

2 tablespoons water

2 large eggs

TOPPING

½ cup unsalted butter, melted

1 ½ cups confectioners' sugar

3 tablespoons crème de menthe liqueur

1 ½ cups bittersweet chocolate

5 tablespoons unsalted butter

Yield: 48 small bars

Preheat the oven to 325 degrees. Grease a 9 × 13-inch pan.

TO MAKE THE BROWNIES: In a small bowl, stir together the flour, baking soda, and salt.

In a large bowl, combine the chocolate chips and vanilla.

In a saucepan, combine the butter, sugar, and water. Bring this mixture to a boil. Pour the hot mixture over the chips and stir. Add the eggs one at a time, mixing well after each addition. Stir in the flour mixture. Pour the mixture into the prepared pan. Spread the mixture evenly. The brownies will appear thin, but this is OK.

Bake the brownies for 15 minutes, or until they are slightly firm to the touch. A toothpick inserted should not be clean. It should still have a very moist crumb on it.

Cool the brownies before spreading the topping on them.

TO MAKE THE TOPPING: Mix the melted butter and confectioners' sugar. Add the crème de menthe. Let it cool and then spread it over the brownies.

Melt the chocolate and remaining tablespoons of butter in a small saucepan or in a small bowl in the microwave, making sure you stir the mixture to prevent burning.

Pour the chocolate mixture over the mint topping and spread it evenly. Cool the brownies completely and cut into squares.

Beach Brownies

I often bring Tate's chocolate chip cookies to the beach to use with roasted marshmallows. This saves going to the supermarket for chocolate and graham crackers to make s'mores, and the combination is even more delicious. Another fun variation is chocolate chip cookies with roasted marshmallows. You don't even need the fire for this one, but I think that the fire-roasted exterior really is the best part of the marshmallow.

Preheat the oven to 350 degrees.

TO MAKE THE BASE: In a small bowl, combine the graham cracker crumbs and melted butter. Spoon the mixture into a glass 9 × 13-inch pan and pat down evenly to cover the bottom only. Set it aside. (I like to line the bottom with aluminum foil, leaving a 3-inch overhang on the short side of the pan. I can then lift out the entire brownie so that I can cut it very cleanly.)

TO MAKE THE BROWNIES: In a medium saucepan, heat the butter and sugar, stirring constantly until the sugar and butter are melted.

In a large bowl, add the chocolate chips. Pour the hot sugar mixture over the chocolate chips and stir it till it is melted. Add the vanilla and mix. Beat in the eggs, one at a time.

In a medium bowl, mix the flour and salt together. Add the flour mixture to the chocolate mixture and stir until they are just combined. Stir in the milk chocolate.

Pour mixture into a prepared pan and spread it evenly. Place the marshmallows, cut side down, evenly over the top. Try to arrange it so that each brownie has a marshmallow half on it.

Bake the brownies for 35 minutes, or until they are slightly firm to the touch. Do not overbake.

Let the brownies cool, and then cut them.

GRAHAM CRACKER BASE

2 cups graham cracker crumbs

7 tablespoons salted butter, melted

BROWNIE

1 cup salted butter

1 1/2 cups sugar

3 1/2 cups semisweet chocolate chips

1 tablespoon vanilla

5 large eggs

1 1/2 cups all-purpose flour

1/4 teaspoon salt

4 ounces milk chocolate, chopped

12 large marshmallows, cut in half

Yield: 24 brownies

Kara's Blondie Brownies

My eighteen-year-old niece Kara Driscoll is an exceptional baker, as my nephew Nate re-minded me daily the summer he spent with me in 2004. He always told me she was better at baking than I am. Still, Nate ate everything I made, so, hopefully, I am not that far behind Kara! She developed this recipe from one in my first book, by layering the brownie and blondie recipes. I think it's a very creative idea.

✎

BLONDIES

2 1/4 cups all-purpose flour
1 teaspoon baking powder
1/4 teaspoon salt
1 cup salted butter, softened
  to room temperature
1 3/4 cups firmly packed light
  brown sugar
2 large eggs
2 teaspoons vanilla
1 cup chopped pecans
1 cup semisweet chocolate
  chips

BROWNIES

3/4 cup all-purpose flour
1/4 teaspoon baking soda
1/4 teaspoon salt
2 cups semisweet chocolate
  chips
1 teaspoon vanilla
1/3 cup salted butter
2/3 cup granulated sugar
2 tablespoons water
2 large eggs

Yield: 24 bars

Preheat the oven to 350 degrees. Grease a 9 × 13-inch baking pan.

TO MAKE THE BLONDIES: In a large bowl, stir together the flour, baking powder, and salt.

In another large bowl, cream the butter and sugar until they are light and fluffy. Beat in the eggs, one at a time, until they are well blended. Mix in the vanilla. Stir in the flour mixture until it is well blended. Scrape down the sides of the bowl. Fold in the pecans and chocolate chips. Spread the batter evenly in the prepared pan. Set it aside.

NOTE: Use a 9-inch square pan if you just want to make blondies.

TO MAKE THE BROWNIES: In a small bowl, stir together the flour, baking soda, and salt.

In a large bowl, combine the chocolate chips and vanilla.

In a saucepan, combine the butter, sugar, and water. Bring the mixture just to a boil. Pour the hot mixture over the chips and stir them until they are melted. Add the eggs one at a time, mixing well after each addition. Stir in the flour mixture and mix it till it is just combined.

Pour the mixture over the blondie mixture and spread it evenly.

Bake the brownies for 30 to 35 minutes, or until an inserted toothpick comes out with a moist crumb. You don't want to over-bake these brownies. When they are cool, cut them into squares.

White Chocolate Brownies

These brownies are not as fudgy as a chocolate brownie; they are more like a dense, yummy vanilla bar with cranberries and almonds. They are a beautiful addition to your Christmas favorites—or anytime, actually!

9 tablespoons salted butter, cut into pieces

9 ounces white chocolate, chopped small

1 tablespoon vanilla

1 ½ cups all-purpose flour

¾ teaspoon baking powder

¼ teaspoon salt

3 large eggs

¾ cup sugar

1 cup dried cranberries

½ cup almonds, chopped

Yield: 16 brownies

Preheat the oven to 325 degrees. Spray and place waxed paper in a 9-inch-square baking pan.

In a small pot, combine the butter and white chocolate. Over low heat, melt the butter and chocolate slowly. Remove the pot from heat and let it cool to room temperature. Add the vanilla.

In a small bowl, mix the flour, baking powder, and salt.

In a large bowl with an electric mixer, beat the eggs and sugar until they are thick and pale. Add the white chocolate mixture and mix till it is combined. Add the flour mixture and mix it till it is combined.

Stir in the cranberries and almonds.

Pour the mixture into the prepared pan and spread it evenly.

Bake for 45 minutes, or until a cake tester or toothpick comes out clean. Do not underbake these brownies as you might a traditional brownie or they will taste raw.

Refrigerate the brownies overnight. Remove them from the pan and cut them into squares.

Raspberry Squares

These raspberry squares were featured on the Food Network show $40.00 a Day. Make sure you use a high-quality raspberry jam, like Clearbrook Farms, because it really makes all the difference.

Preheat the oven to 350 degrees. Grease a 9-inch-square baking pan.

In a large bowl, cream the butter and sugar until they are combined. Add the egg yolk and mix. Add the flour and almonds and blend them well, but keep the mixture a bit crumbly, and not too dry.

Pat half the mixture, about 3 cups, into the prepared pan. Bake it for 20 minutes. Remove it from the oven and immediately spread it with raspberry jam, leaving about a ¼-inch border along the sides.

Crumble the remaining dough evenly over the jam. Pat lightly. Bake it for another 40 minutes. The bars should be golden brown on top.

1 cup salted butter, softened to room temperature
1 cup sugar
1 egg yolk
3 cups all-purpose flour
1 cup whole almonds, chopped
1 ¼ cups raspberry jam

Yield: 16 squares

Magic Bars

This is an old-style cookie bar from the 1930s, but I made this version a little more adult by using unsweetened coconut and Scharffen Berger chocolate chunks. When my nephew first tried them and I told him they were magic bars, his response was "What? Gain five pounds magically overnight?"

½ cup salted butter, melted

1 ½ cups graham cracker crumbs

1 ⅓ cups desiccated shaved coconut (unsweetened), (can be found at most health food stores)

1 ½ cups bittersweet chocolate chunks

1 ¼ cups pecans, chopped

1 can (14 ounces) sweetened condensed milk

Yield: 24 bars

Preheat the oven to 350 degrees.

In a 9 × 13-inch pan, mix the melted butter and graham cracker crumbs. Press the mixture evenly to cover the bottom of the pan.

Sprinkle the coconut over the crumb base.

Sprinkle the chocolate chunks over the coconut.

Sprinkle the pecans over the chocolate chunks.

Drizzle sweetened condensed milk evenly over the top.

Bake it for 25 minutes.

Cool it completely and cut it into bars. I like these magic bars served cold.

Dot's Lemon Bars

Dot Dalsimer, a friend who passed on a couple of years ago at age eighty-six, gave me this recipe. She always said her lemon bars were better than mine! Dot was the youngest eighty-six-year-old I have ever met. When I asked her the secret of her youth, she replied, "Keep getting younger friends."

Preheat the oven to 350 degrees.

TO MAKE THE BASE: In a medium bowl, mix the butter, flour, and sugar with your hands till the mixture is well blended. Place the mixture in a 9 × 13-inch pan. Pat the mixture evenly on the bottom of the pan. Bake for 30 minutes.

TO MAKE THE TOPPING: While the base is baking, beat the eggs. Add the sugar and lemon zest. Mix thoroughly. Add the flour and mix it till it is incorporated.

When the base is baked, remove the pan from the oven. Add the lemon juice to the sugar mixture and mix. Pour it over the warm base and bake it for 20 minutes.

When it is cool, cut it into squares. Dust it with more confectioners' sugar, if desired. Admittedly, the lemon bars look prettier sugared, but I prefer them plain.

BASE

1 cup salted butter, softened
   to room temperature
2 cups all-purpose flour
½ cup confectioners' sugar

LEMON TOPPING

4 large eggs
1¾ cups sugar
Grated zest of 1 lemon
4 tablespoons all-purpose
   flour
½ cup lemon juice

Yield: 16 squares

Cream Cheese Brownies

We sell hundreds of cream cheese brownies at Tate's Bake Shop. When you can't decide between chocolate and cheesecake, this recipe will satisfy both cravings.

&

1 ½ cups semisweet
    chocolate chips
1 pound cream cheese, room
    temperature
1 ¾ cups sugar
4 large eggs at room
    temperature
3 teaspoons vanilla
1 cup salted butter, softened
    to room temperature
1 cup all-purpose flour
¼ teaspoon salt

Yield: 16 brownies

Preheat the oven to 350 degrees.

Line a 9-inch-square baking pan with aluminum foil so that the foil extends two inches beyond the sides of the pan. (This creates handles you can use to remove the brownies later.) Spray it with nonstick cooking spray.

Melt the chocolate in a small saucepan over low heat. Set it aside to cool.

In a large bowl, using an electric mixer, beat the cream cheese and ¼ cup of the sugar until they are smooth. Beat in one egg and 1 teaspoon of the vanilla until they are combined. Set it aside.

In a large bowl, using an electric mixer, beat the butter and remaining 1 ½ cups sugar until they are combined. Beat in the remaining 3 eggs, one at a time. Beat in the remaining 2 teaspoons of vanilla. Mix in the melted chocolate. On low speed, beat in the flour and salt until they are just combined.

Scrape all but 1 cup of the chocolate batter into the prepared pan and smooth it out evenly. Spread the cream cheese mixture evenly over the chocolate mixture. Spoon the remaining chocolate mixture over the cream cheese mixture. Pull a table knife though the layers of batter with a light lifting motion in a zigzag pattern to create a marbleized look.

Bake it for 50 minutes.

Set the pan on a wire rack and cool the brownies in the pan.

When the brownies are completely cool, remove them using the aluminum foil handles.

Cut them into squares. (I like to refrigerate them first for ease of cutting. Wetting your knife also helps give you a clean cut.)

OPTIONAL: Add a half pint of raspberries to the cream cheese mixture by pressing them into the topping before adding the final chocolate layer and baking. This is a great variation on a basic recipe.

Hermits

This recipe comes from my Aunt Cordelia, who has always been an excellent baker. It makes an old-style bar cookie that is sweet, spicy, and chewy. It reminds me of the tastes of fall.

2 cups all-purpose flour
1/4 teaspoon baking soda
1/4 teaspoon salt
1 teaspoon cinnamon
3/4 teaspoon ground cloves
3/4 cup vegetable shortening
1 cup sugar
1 large egg
1/4 cup dark molasses
1 cup raisins, dark or golden

Yield: 35 cookie bars

Preheat the oven to 325 degrees. Grease two cookie sheets or line them with Silpat.

In a small bowl, combine the flour, baking soda, salt, cinnamon, and cloves.

Cream the vegetable shortening and sugar till they are combined. Add the egg and molasses, and mix them until they are combined. Scrape down the sides of the bowl and mix them again.

Add the flour mixture and mix it till it's just combined. Add the raisins and mix them until they are combined.

Roll the dough into 7 equal logs. Do this with your hands as if you were handling clay. The logs should be about 7 inches long and 1½ inches wide. Place the logs on the 2 prepared cookie sheets.

Bake the logs for 20 minutes.

Remove the logs from the oven and let them cool for 5 minutes. Cut them into bars, approximately 5 per log.

Passover Brownies

I was invited to my first Passover dinner in 2004. I created this brownie as a dessert for the kids, but I think the adults loved them even more. They are very simple, fudgy, and dense. They keep well in the refrigerator.

❧

Preheat the oven to 350 degrees.

Prepare a 9-inch square pan with nonstick spray and waxed paper liner on the bottom. (I like to use waxed paper so I can easily remove the brownies to cut them more evenly.)

Mix the espresso powder and water. Set it aside.

In a medium bowl, mix the sugars into the melted butter until they are combined. Add the eggs, coffee mixture, cocoa, salt, and matzoh meal.

Pour the mixture into the prepared pan and smooth the batter evenly.

Bake the batter for 30 minutes. Do not overbake it. The center should still be a bit soft.

Cool the brownies in the pan. Loosen the edges and remove them from the pan. Cut them into squares.

1/2 teaspoon espresso powder
1 tablespoon hot water
1 cup white sugar
3/4 cup firmly packed dark or light brown sugar
1 cup unsalted kosher butter, melted (for a lighter brownies, substitute 1/2 cup applesauce for 1/2 cup of the butter)
3 large eggs
3/4 cup unsweetened Dutch-processed cocoa powder, sifted
1/4 teaspoon salt
1 cup, minus 2 tablespoons, matzoh meal

Yield: 16 brownies

Peanut Butter Squares

This bar is more like a candy and resembles the best-tasting peanut butter cup you will ever eat! They keep for a couple of weeks in the refrigerator, and there is no baking involved.

⅗

¾ cup firmly packed dark or light brown sugar

3 cups confectioners' sugar

½ cup salted butter, softened to room temperature

2 cups smooth peanut butter

2 cups semisweet chocolate chips

1 tablespoon salted butter

Yield: 40 two-inch squares

In a large bowl, combine the brown sugar, confectioners' sugar, butter, and peanut butter, and beat them with an electric mixer until they are smooth and well blended. Pat into an ungreased 15½ × 10½ × 1-inch pan. Roll the mixture flat on top with a rolling pin.

Melt the chocolate chips and butter in the top of a double boiler or in the microwave. Spread the chocolate mixture over the peanut butter mixture and cut into squares while the chocolate is still warm and soft.

Chill the mixture for about 15 minutes and remove the squares from the pan.

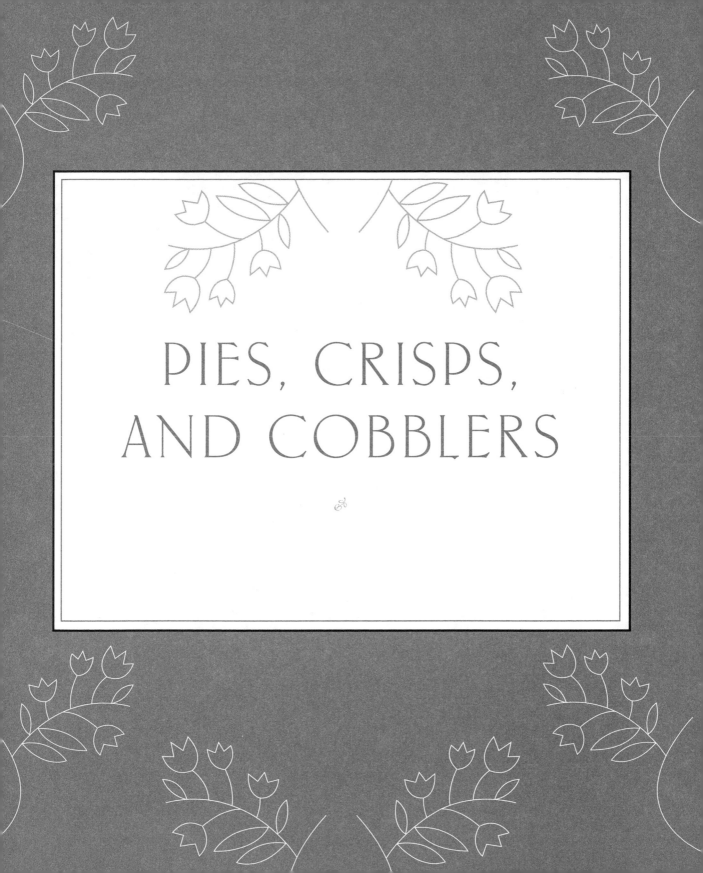

PIES, CRISPS, AND COBBLERS

Pear Crisp

Pears are readily available all year long, but in the fall, fresh from the orchard, they are exceptional. Pear crisp is easy to put together and is best served warm. Place it in the oven before your guests arrive for dinner and serve it just out of the oven for dessert with vanilla or ginger ice cream.

⚜

Preheat the oven to 375 degrees. Grease a 9-inch-square pan or a 9-inch deep-dish glass pie plate.

TO MAKE THE PEAR MIXTURE: In a large bowl, combine the brown sugar, ginger, lemon juice, nutmeg, and flour. Add the pears and toss them gently in the mixture. Spoon the pear mixture into the prepared pan and set it aside.

TO MAKE THE CRUMB TOPPING: In a small bowl, combine the flour, sugar, walnuts, and butter. Blend them until the mixture is crumbly.

Top the fruit evenly with the crumb mixture. Place the pan on a cookie sheet to catch any drippings.

Bake it for 1 hour or until the crumb topping starts to brown and the fruit is bubbly.

PEAR MIXTURE

1/4 cup firmly packed dark or
   light brown sugar
1/4 cup crystallized ginger,
   minced
2 tablespoons fresh lemon
   juice, from one lemon
1/4 teaspoon nutmeg
1/4 cup all-purpose flour
5 cups peeled and cored
   sliced pears

CRUMB TOPPING

1/3 cup all-purpose flour
1/4 cup sugar
3/4 cup ground walnuts
6 tablespoons salted butter,
   chilled

Yield: 1 nine-inch crisp

Rhubarb Cobbler

This cobbler is a very homey, not too sweet dessert. It really lets the rhubarb flavor shine through.

⸙

4 cups rhubarb, cut into
 ½-inch lengths
½ cup sugar
2 cups cake flour, sifted
¾ teaspoon baking powder
½ cup sugar
½ cup salted butter, cold,
 cut into pieces
⅓ cup heavy cream
1 large egg
1 egg yolk
1 teaspoon vanilla

Yield: 8 servings

Preheat the oven to 400 degrees. Butter a 10-inch glass pie plate or oval gratin dish.

Mix the rhubarb with the sugar. Spoon it into the prepared dish.

In a medium bowl, mix the flour, baking powder, and sugar until they are combined. Blend in the butter with a pastry knife until the mixture resembles coarse meal.

Whisk together the cream, whole egg, egg yolk, and vanilla. Add it to the dry ingredients and mix them lightly. Spoon the dough on top of the rhubarb mixture. It will be rough looking, and that is what you want.

Bake it for 30 minutes or until the biscuit is golden brown and the fruit is bubbling.

Cool it 20 minutes before serving.

Serve it with whipped cream or ice cream (vanilla, of course, but strawberry or ginger would be delicious, too).

Tart Pastry

While attending a course given by the famous chocolatier Albert Kumin, I met a woman who raved about her tart crust. She gave me this recipe and I recently found it scribbled on a little Marriott notepad. When I tasted the tart, I was so glad I never lost that little piece of paper.

❧

Mix the egg yolk and cream. Set it aside.

Mix the sugar, flour, and butter till they are crumbly.

Combine the egg mixture with the flour mixture, using a fork, and mix them till they are just combined. Form the dough into a disk and wrap it in clear film. Refrigerate it for at least 1 hour.

Roll it out ⅛-inch thick and place it in a 9-inch round tart pan with a removable bottom.

Prick the bottom all over with a fork. At this point, you can place it in the refrigerator for later use, freeze it for future use, or bake it right away. (I always keep prepared tart shells and piecrust in the freezer for future use. This is a big time-saver.)

Bake it at 350 degrees for 30 minutes or until it is golden brown.

1 large egg yolk
2 tablespoons cream
2 tablespoons sugar
1 ½ cups all-purpose flour
½ cup salted butter, chilled
and cut into pieces

Yield: 1 nine-inch tart pastry

Rhubarb Tart

A beautiful rustic tart for rhubarb purists. Rhubarb tart is best served the same day it is made because the crust tends to get a bit soggy overnight. Prepare the tart shell in advance, and it will only take minutes to finish this recipe up.

⁂

Tart dough (recipe on page 71) for a 9-inch round pan with a removable bottom
3½ cups rhubarb, cut into ¼-inch lengths
¼ cup sugar
1 tablespoon sugar
1 tablespoon salted butter

Yield: 1 nine-inch tart

TO PREPARE THE TART DOUGH: Pierce the bottom of the dough with a fork if you have not already done so. Wrap the tart shell and refrigerate it for at least 30 minutes. Or make it a day ahead and keep it refrigerated, or pull one from the freezer if you have made them well in advance.

Preheat the oven to 425 degrees.

TO MAKE THE RHUBARB FILLING: Combine the rhubarb and ¼ cup sugar in a medium bowl. Sprinkle the tart shell with 1 tablespoon sugar. Fill it with the rhubarb mixture and spread it evenly. Dot the top with small pieces of butter.

Bake it for 40 minutes or until the tart shell is brown and the fruit is bubbling.

Cool before serving.

Buttermilk Pie Crust

I am always searching for a better pie crust recipe, and this one is my latest favorite. It is consistently good and easy to roll. Use it for double-crust pie, single crusts, and gallettes.

In a large bowl, combine the flour, sugar, and salt. Add the butter and vegetable shortening. Cut them in using your hands or a pastry blender. (I am a hands person, but I prefer a pastry blender or two knives to cut in butter and shortening.) Blend it till the mixture resembles a coarse meal the size of peas.

Add the buttermilk and mix it until the mixture is just moistened. You don't want it wet.

Press the dough together and divide it in half. Wrap each piece in clear film and chill it for 1 hour.

Roll out one half of the dough on a lightly floured surface, in a circle 3 inches larger than the pie pan you plan on using. Fit the round dough into the pie pan and either flute the edges by turning the excess underneath around the edges on the rim, or leave as is for a double-crust pie.

For a top crust, roll out the second half the same size and shape and place it over the filling. Seal the edges; trim and flute the dough.

TO PREBAKE THE PIE SHELL: Prick the bottom of the crust with a fork to vent it. Use a piece of aluminum foil to cover the bottom and sides of the pastry, forming the same inside shape. Fill the inside with small dried beans. (These can be used over and over again.) Bake it in a preheated oven at 400 degrees for 15 minutes. Remove the foil and beans, reprick the bottom crust, and continue baking until it is golden brown.

NOTE: This crust recipe can be used for many of the following pie recipes.

2½ cups all-purpose flour
1 tablespoon sugar
¾ teaspoon salt
½ cup salted butter, chilled and cut into small pieces
½ cup vegetable shortening, chilled and cut into small pieces
6 tablespoons buttermilk, chilled

Yield: 2 nine-inch single crusts or 1 nine-inch double crust

Nancy Hardy's Pecan Pie

Nancy is a lovely southern woman who shops at Tate's Bake Shop often, even though she is a great baker herself. She always claims her pecan pie is better than mine!

9-inch pie shell (recipe on page 73), unbaked

3 large eggs
½ cup sugar
1 cup corn syrup
1 teaspoon vanilla
1 tablespoon salted butter melted
1 cup pecans, chopped

Yield: 1 nine-inch pie

Preheat the oven to 350 degrees.

Prepare a pie shell and set it aside.

Mix the eggs, sugar, corn syrup, vanilla, and butter.

Place the pecans in the bottom of the prepared pie shell. Pour the egg mixture over the pecans.

Bake the pie for 45 minutes or until it is set in the middle.

Apricot Cherry Pie

Apricots and Bing cherries are in season at the same time, so I guess they were just meant to go together!

Preheat the oven to 400 degrees.

Roll out the pie pastry in a deep-dish 9-inch glass pie plate. Brush the inside with a beaten egg white to prevent the crust from becoming soggy.

In a large bowl, mix the apricots, cherries, lemon zest, ginger, sugar, flour, and almond extract.

Spoon the mixture into the prepared pie crust. Top the fruit with the butter pieces. Roll out the top crust and cover the fruit. Seal the edges and crimp the rim as desired. Place the pie on a sheet pan to catch the drippings.

Bake the pie for 1 hour 20 minutes or until the crust is golden brown and the fruit is bubbling.

Pie pastry for a double 9-inch crust (recipe on page 73)

1 large egg white, beaten

4 cups fresh apricots, pitted and cut in 1/4-inch slices

2 cups Bing cherries, pitted

Zest from 1 lemon

2 tablespoons crystallized ginger (optional)

1/2 cup sugar

1/4 cup all-purpose flour

1/4 teaspoon almond extract

2 tablespoons salted butter, cut into pieces

Yield: 1 nine-inch pie

Peach Pie

My friend Karen Lanza kept trying to make me sell this pie in the shop, but I explained that I would have to charge $30 for it. She said she would be first in line, even at that price! I still don't make a $30 peach pie, but I do make the pie for Karen as a surprise treat during peach season.

⚓

Double 9-inch pie crust
  (recipe on page 73)
I egg white, beaten

8 cups fresh peaches,
  peeled, pitted, and sliced
  (about 4 pounds)
½ cup sugar
5 tablespoons all-purpose
  flour
I teaspoon vanilla
½ teaspoon cinnamon
¼ teaspoon ginger
¼ teaspoon nutmeg

Yield: 1 nine-inch pie

Preheat the oven to 400 degrees.

Roll out 1 disk of pie dough to a 12- to 13-inch round. Transfer it to a deep-dish 9-inch glass pie pan. Brush the bottom with the beaten egg white to prevent the crust from becoming soggy.

Combine the peaches, sugar, flour, vanilla, cinnamon, ginger, and nutmeg in a large bowl. Toss the peaches till they are evenly coated.

Fill the pie pan with the peach mixture.

Roll out a second disk of pie dough 12 to 13 inches in diameter and place it on top of the peaches. Seal the edges, trim, and flute as desired.

Make 4 vents in the top crust with a knife. Place the pie on a cookie sheet to catch the drips.

Bake the pie for one hour or until the crust is golden and the fruit mixture is bubbling. Remove the pie pan to a wire rack and cool it. Serve the pie warm (or cold), but not hot.

Open-Faced Fresh Blueberry Tart

My favorite summer fruit is blueberries. In this pie half of the blueberries are cooked and the rest are folded in. The cinnamon boosts the flavor of the fruit without shouting its presence.

In a medium saucepan, mix the sugar, cornstarch, and salt. Mix them well. Add the cold water and mix it well. Add 1 cup of blueberries. Cook the mixture over low heat until it thickens and the blueberries start to pop. Remove it from the heat.

Stir in the cinnamon, butter, and lemon juice.

Stir in the remaining blueberries and spoon the mixture into a prebaked tart shell or pie shell.

One prebaked tart shell
   (recipe on page 71) or pie
   shell (recipe on page 73)

½ cup sugar
2½ tablespoons cornstarch
Pinch of salt
⅔ cup cold water
4 cups fresh blueberries

¼ teaspoon cinnamon
2 tablespoons salted butter
1½ tablespoons lemon juice

Yield: 1 nine-inch tart or pie

Rhubarb Pie

When my brother Richie first introduced his wife, Robin, to the family, she brought this rhubarb pie along. She and her recipe have now been in the family for twenty-five years!

Pie pastry for a double-crust 9-inch pie (recipe on page 73)

1 large egg white, beaten

6 tablespoons flour
1 ½ cups sugar
2 large eggs
4 cups rhubarb, cut in ¼-inch pieces

Yield: 1 nine-inch pie

Preheat the oven to 425 degrees.

Roll out the pie pastry for a 9-inch glass pie plate. Brush the inside of the pastry shell with the beaten egg white to prevent it from becoming soggy.

Stir the flour and sugar together. Add the eggs and beat them in by hand. Stir in the rhubarb.

Pour the mixture into the prepared pie shell. Roll out a piecrust to cover the top and cut in 4 slits to vent the steam. Place the pie on a cookie sheet to catch any drips.

Bake the pie for 1 hour or until the crust is golden brown and the fruit is bubbling.

Chocolate Wafer Cookie Crust

Chocolate Wafer Cookie Crust is an easy, no-bake crust that is versatile enough to be used in many different pies. This is the perfect crust for you if the idea of making a pastry stresses you out. This crust also can be frozen for later use.

Melt the butter.

In a small bowl, combine the chocolate wafer crumbs and melted butter. Mix them well.

Press the mixture into a 9-inch-deep glass pie plate to form the piecrust.

2 cups chocolate wafer crumbs or Oreo cookie crumbs
6 tablespoons salted butter

Yield: 1 nine-inch piecrust

Crème de Menthe Pie

When I was a kid, this crème de menthe pie was called grasshopper pie because it was always bright green. I prefer to use clear crème de menthe. This was definitely one of my favorite kid desserts. Even though I am not a kid anymore, I still love it!

9-inch Chocolate Wafer
  Cookie Crust (recipe on
  page 79)

¼ cup milk
¼ cup crème de menthe
1 7½-ounce jar of
  marshmallow fluff
1 cup heavy cream

Yield: 1 nine-inch pie

In a medium bowl, mix the milk, crème de menthe, and marshmallow fluff with a wire whisk. Mix it until it is smooth and well combined.

In a separate bowl, beat the heavy cream till it is thick and fold it into the milk mixture.

Pour the mixture into the prepared crust, smooth the top, and freeze.

This pie is served frozen.

Gingersnap Crumb Crust

Gingersnap Crumb Crust is similar to a graham cracker crust, but has more zip. Use this recipe for tarts, cheesecake bases, and pie shells, or for Lemon Cream Cheese Tart (recipe on page 82)

Preheat the oven to 375 degrees.

In a food processor, grind the gingersnaps to yield 2 cups.

In a medium bowl, combine the gingersnap crumbs and melted butter. Stir them till they are well combined. (Sometimes I use my hands at the end so that all the butter is incorporated well, but you can use a wooden spoon.)

Dump the crumb mixture into a 10-inch tart pan with a removable bottom and pat it evenly onto the sides and bottom.

Place the tart pan on a cookie sheet and bake the crust for 10 minutes.

Cool the crust and use it with the lemon cream cheese filling (recipe on page 82) or any other recipe that catches your fancy.

2 cups ground gingersnaps
7 tablespoons salted butter, melted

Yield: 1 ten-inch tart shell

Lemon Cream Cheese Tart

I love traditional lemon curd tarts, but the addition of cream cheese and whipped cream makes this one fantastic. For a quick dessert, fold the lemon curd into the whipped cream, leaving streaks, and use it on fresh fruit instead of plain whipped cream. There are many good commercial lemon curds you can substitute if you want to omit that step in order to save time.

10-inch prebaked
  Gingersnap Crumb Crust
  (recipe on page 81)

LEMON CURD

8 large egg yolks
1 cup sugar
¾ cup fresh lemon juice,
  strained
Grated zest from one lemon
½ cup salted butter cut into
  small pieces

CREAM CHEESE
FILLING

8 ounces cream cheese,
  softened to room
  temperature
⅓ cup sugar
1 teaspoon vanilla
1 cup heavy cream

Yield: 1 ten-inch tart

TO MAKE THE LEMON CURD: In the top of a double boiler, combine the egg yolks, sugar, lemon juice, and lemon zest. Whisk until the ingredients are well blended. Add the butter pieces.

Place the top of the double boiler over simmering water in the bottom half. Cook the mixture, whisking constantly, until the butter is melted and the mixture is thickened and coats the back of a spoon. This will take about 8 minutes. Make sure that the water in the double boiler stays at a simmer.

Remove the top from the bottom of the double boiler and transfer the curd to a small bowl. Press a sheet of clear plastic film on top of the lemon curd to prevent a skin from forming. Refrigerate it for several hours or overnight.

TO MAKE THE CREAM CHEESE FILLING: Whip the cream cheese and sugar till they are very soft and creamy. Add the vanilla and stir. Set it aside.

Beat the heavy cream till it forms stiff peaks.

Fold the whipped cream into the cream cheese mixture.

Fold 2 cups of the cream cheese mixture into the chilled lemon curd.

Spoon the mixture into the prepared tart shell and spread it evenly.

Put the remaining cream cheese mixture in a pastry bag and pipe out rosettes around the rim of the tart as a decoration and to mark each slice. This is not necessary, and you can just fold the entire mixture into the lemon curd if you like. Whatever you feel like doing is fine.

Apple Cream Cheese Tart

I love the flavor of cream cheese combined with apples. This tart is an exceptional, effort-less dessert. I like making it in the fall with the Golden Delicious apples from the Milk Pail in Water Mill.

9-inch pie crust, three-quarters baked (recipe on page 73)

APPLE TOPPING

1 ½ apples, peeled, cored, and sliced thin, about ⅛-inch
1 tablespoon lemon juice from ½ fresh lemon
1 tablespoon vanilla
1 tablespoon Grand Marnier
¼ cup sugar
1 teaspoon cinnamon

CREAM CHEESE FILLING

8 ounces cream cheese, softened to room temperature
⅓ cup sugar
1 large egg
2 teaspoons vanilla

Yield: 1 nine-inch tart

TO MAKE THE APPLE TOPPING: In a small bowl, combine the apples, lemon juice, vanilla, Grand Marnier, sugar, and cinnamon. Set the mixture aside for 30 minutes.

Preheat the oven to 350 degrees.

TO MAKE THE CREAM CHEESE FILLING: Place the cream cheese and sugar in a food processor or in an electric mixer, and process them till they are smooth. Add the egg and vanilla, scrape down the bowl, and process it till the mixture is smooth and without lumps.

Pour the filling into the prepared crust. Fan out the seasoned apple slices all around the perimeter of the tart and in the center. Pour any remaining juices from the bowl evenly over the tart.

Place the tart on a sheet pan and bake it for 35 to 40 minutes or until the apples are soft, and the center is just set.

Cool the tart and serve it at room temperature or chilled.

Blueberry Pie

This perfectly simple blueberry pie has just the right sweetness and flavor to enhance the fruit and not kill it.

Preheat the oven to 375 degrees.

Roll out the pie pastry for the bottom crust. Brush it with the beaten egg white to prevent the crust from becoming soggy and set it aside.

In a large bowl, stir together the sugar, flour, and cinnamon. Add the blueberries and toss them together.

Sprinkle the lemon juice over the fruit and dot it with butter.

Cover the mixture with the top crust, seal the edges by pressing gently around the rim, trim the excess dough, and flute it as desired.

Make four vents in the top with a knife. Place the pie on a cookie sheet to catch any drips.

Bake the pie for 1 hour or until the crust is golden and the filling bubbly.

Remove the pan to a wire rack and cool the pie completely before serving it. The pie will be too runny if it is sliced hot.

Pie pastry for a double-crust 9-inch pie (recipe on page 73)
1 egg white, beaten

½ cup white sugar
5 tablespoons all-purpose flour
½ teaspoon cinnamon
4–5 cups fresh or frozen blueberries
1 tablespoon fresh lemon juice, about ½ lemon
2 tablespoons salted butter

Yield: 1 nine-inch pie

Sweet Potato Pie

Sweet potato pie is similar to pumpkin pie, but the texture is slightly different, and it has an overall more mellow taste and texture. If you have never tasted it before, I think you will welcome it as a nice change from pumpkin pie.

❧

9-inch unbaked pie crust
  (recipe on page 73)

1 ½ cups mashed sweet
  potatoes or yams
½ cup salted butter,
  softened to room
  temperature
¾ cup sugar
1 5-ounce can evaporated
  milk, or ½ cup plus 2
  tablespoons
2 large eggs
½ teaspoon nutmeg
½ teaspoon cinnamon
1 teaspoon vanilla

Yield: 1 nine-inch pie

Bake the sweet potatoes at 400 degrees until they are soft and easily pierced by a fork. Remove them from the oven and split them open until they are cool enough to handle. Remove the skin and mash the potatoes. Measure out 1½ cups (about 1 pound of whole sweet potatoes). This step can be done in advance.

Preheat the oven to 350 degrees.

In a medium bowl, mix the sweet potatoes and softened butter until they are smooth. Stir in the sugar, evaporated milk, eggs, nutmeg, cinnamon, and vanilla. Beat the ingredients with an electric mixer until the mixture is smooth.

Pour the filling into the prepared pie crust.

Bake the pie for 1 hour or until the filling feels firm when lightly pressed with a fingertip.

Apricot Pie

For two years, my friend Roberto, a good customer of Tate's, asked me to make him a fresh apricot pie like our apple pie, which is not too sweet. Each year the apricot season passed, and so did the opportunity to make the pie. Finally, the apricots and Roberto were in Southampton at the same time, and he finally got his pie. It is not very sweet, but can be adjusted to your taste by adding a bit more sugar.

Preheat the oven to 400 degrees.

Roll out the pastry for a bottom crust to fit a 9-inch pie plate. Brush the bottom with the beaten egg white to prevent the crust from becoming soggy.

Prepare the apricots and place them in a large bowl. Add the sugar, flour, lemon juice, and cinnamon, and toss them together to coat the fruit.

Place the apricot mixture into the prepared crust and dot it with butter.

Roll out the top crust and place it over the apricots. Seal the rim and vent the top with four slits. Place the pie on a cookie sheet to catch any drips.

Bake the pie for 50 minutes or until the crust is golden brown and the fruit is bubbling.

Cool the pie. I prefer this apricot pie at room temperature instead of warm.

Pastry for a double-crust 9-inch pie (recipe on page 73)
1 large egg white, beaten

4 cups apricots, peeled by hand, pitted, and cut in half
2/3 cup sugar
1/4 cup all-purpose flour
1 tablespoon lemon juice
1/2 teaspoon cinnamon
2 tablespoons salted butter

Yield: 1 nine-inch pie

Chocolate Peanut Butter Pie

This pie is like a giant Reese's Peanut Butter Cup, but even more creamy and decadent! When my friend Sam Eber stopped by to visit just after I made this, he ate two pieces on the spot—and took the rest of the pie home.

CRUST

1 prepared Chocolate Wafer Cookie Crust (recipe on page 79)

FILLING

12 ounces cream cheese

1 ½ cups creamy peanut butter

1 cup sugar

½ teaspoon vanilla

1 cup heavy cream

TOPPING

2 tablespoons sugar

½ cup heavy cream

2 ounces bittersweet chocolate

4 tablespoons salted butter

½ teaspoon vanilla

½ cup chopped peanuts (optional)

Yield: 1 nine-inch pie

Preheat the oven to 350 degrees.

TO PREPARE THE CRUST: Bake the crust for 10 minutes. Set it aside and cool it completely.

TO MAKE THE FILLING: With an electric mixer, mix the cream cheese, peanut butter, sugar, and vanilla together in a large bowl until they are light and airy. In a separate bowl, beat the cream until it is stiff. Fold the cream into the cream cheese mixture and spoon it into the prepared crust.

TO MAKE THE TOPPING: Combine the sugar and cream in a small saucepan and bring it to a boil. Remove it from the heat and add the chocolate, butter, and vanilla. Stir it until the ingredients are completely combined. Cool the mixture so that it is still pourable, but not too runny.

Slowly pour the topping over the pie and refrigerate it, uncovered, overnight or for at least 4 hours.

Garnish it with chopped peanuts around the rim if you like.

Graham Cracker Crust

Keep these premade pie shells in the freezer to save time when you need a quick dessert. This graham cracker crust also makes a good base for a cheesecake.

Mix the crumbs and sugar in a medium bowl. Add the butter. Stir the mixture till it is well blended. (I prefer to use my hands for this, but you can use a wooden spoon or rubber spatula.) Place the mixture in a 9-inch metal pie pan and press the crumbs evenly against the bottom and sides of the pan. You can freeze the crust at this point. It can be used without baking. If you like your crusts a little crispy, bake it for 10 minutes at 325 degrees, or until the crust starts to brown.

1 1/4 cups graham crackers, processed to fine crumbs, approximately 1 1/2 packets
1 tablespoon sugar
5 tablespoons salted butter, melted

Yield: 1 nine-inch pie crust

Key Lime Pie

We sell hundreds of key lime pies at Tate's Bake Shop. I love the combination of the creamy tart filling and the crunchy graham cracker crust. This recipe is often requested at the shop.

9-inch Graham Cracker
   Crust (recipe on page 89)
4 large egg yolks
1 tablespoon grated lime
   zest, from one lime
1 14-ounce can sweetened
   condensed milk
½ cup fresh lime juice, from
   about 4 limes

Yield: 1 nine-inch pie

Prepare the graham cracker crust in a 9-inch shallow metal pie pan. (Standard glass pie plates are too deep.) Bake the crust for 10 minutes at 325 degrees. Cool it completely.

In a medium bowl, using an electric mixer, beat the yolks and lime zest until they are smooth. Beat in the milk, then slowly pour in the lime juice and beat the mixture continuously until it is smooth.

Pour the filling into the prepared pie shell and bake it at 350 degrees for 10 minutes.

Cool the pie and refrigerate it till it is cold, about 2 hours.

Serve it plain or topped with sweetened whipped cream.

Pumpkin Pie

Pumpkin pie is always the number-one seller at Thanksgiving. Right after Labor Day, the customers at Tate's Bake Shop start requesting pumpkin pie. This version is smooth and creamy and not overly spicy.

Preheat the oven to 350 degrees.

Brush the bottom of the pie shell with the beaten egg white to prevent the crust from becoming soggy. Set it aside.

In a large bowl, beat the eggs. Add the milk and evaporated milk and mix them till they are blended. Add the sugar, cinnamon, ginger, cloves, nutmeg, and salt. Mix the ingredients well. Add the pumpkin and mix the ingredients again. Place the pie shell on a cookie sheet and pour the mixture into the prepared pie shell. (Using the sheet will make it easier to put the pie in the oven without spills.)

Bake the pie for 1 hour or until the filling feels firm when lightly pressed with a fingertip. Remove the pan to a wire rack and let it cool. Serve the pie with whipped cream, if desired.

1 unbaked 9-inch pie shell (recipe on page 73)
1 large egg white, lightly beaten

2 large eggs
2/3 cup milk
1 1/3 cups evaporated milk
1 cup sugar
1 tablespoon cinnamon
1 teaspoon ginger
1/8 teaspoon cloves
1/8 teaspoon nutmeg
1/2 teaspoon salt
2 cups mashed fresh or solid packed pumpkin (Do not use pumpkin pie filling.)

Yield: 1 nine-inch pie

Apple Crumb Pie

The balanced combination of tart filling and sweet crunchy topping in this apple crumb pie is excellent. If you like your pie less sweet, leave off the crumb topping and top the filling with pie pastry for a traditional apple pie.

1 unbaked 9-inch pie shell
(recipe on page 73)

APPLE FILLING

⅓ cup granulated sugar
2 tablespoons all-purpose
   flour
¼ teaspoon nutmeg
¾ teaspoon cinnamon
5 cups apples, peeled, cored,
   and sliced
1 tablespoon lemon juice

CRUMB TOPPING

½ cup all-purpose flour
⅓ cup sugar
4 tablespoons salted butter,
   chilled

Yield: 1 nine-inch pie

Preheat the oven to 375 degrees.

TO MAKE THE APPLE FILLING: Combine the sugar, flour, nutmeg, and cinnamon in a small bowl. Add this spice mixture to the apples and toss the ingredients together. Spoon the apple mixture into the prepared pie shell. Sprinkle the filling with fresh lemon juice and set it aside.

TO MAKE THE CRUMB TOPPING: Combine the flour, sugar, and butter in a small bowl. Using a pastry blender, mix the ingredients until they are crumbly. Sprinkle the crumb topping evenly over the apples.

Bake the pie for 1 hour or until the topping is golden. Remove the pan to a wire rack to let it cool. Serve the pie with vanilla ice cream, if desired.

Strawberry Rhubarb Pie

When the strawberry fields in the Hamptons start producing, the demand for this pie jumps. The combination of sweet and tart fruit with a hint of orange is scrumptious.

Preheat the oven to 400 degrees.

Roll out the bottom crust for a 9-inch pie pan. Brush the crust lightly with egg white to prevent the crust from getting soggy. Set the crust aside.

In a large bowl, stir together the flour, sugar, orange juice, and orange zest. Mix the ingredients well. Fold in the strawberries and rhubarb. Spoon the mixture into the prepared pie shell, and dot the top with butter.

Cover the mixture with the top crust, seal the edges, trim the excess, and flute as desired. Cut a few slits in the top crust to vent. Place the pie on a cookie sheet to catch any drips.

Bake the pie for 1 hour or until the crust is golden. If the edges brown too quickly, cover them with aluminum foil. Remove the pan to a wire rack and cool the pie completely before slicing it. Serve it at room temperature.

Pie pastry for one 9-inch double-crust pie
1 large egg white, lightly beaten

1/3 cup all-purpose flour
1 cup sugar
1/4 cup orange juice
1 teaspoon grated orange zest, from one orange
3 cups cleaned and hulled strawberries
3 cups sliced rhubarb (cut into 1-inch lengths)
1 tablespoon salted butter

Yield: 1 nine-inch pie

Sour Cherry Pie

I made this pie for my friend Thomas Rosamilia, who loves cherries. Buy the cherries while they are in season, pit them, and individually quick-freeze them by laying them on a sheet pan covered in wax paper, then put the whole pan in the freezer. When the fruit is frozen solid, bag it in a Ziploc bag, so that you can save them for that special person when they are in town. Freezing works well with strawberries, blueberries, and most other fruits.

¾ cup sugar

2 tablespoons cornstarch

¼ teaspoon cinnamon

5 cups red tart cherries,
   pitted (thawed, if frozen)

1 tablespoon lemon juice

¼ teaspoon almond extract

1 tablespoon salted butter

Pastry for 9-inch double-
   crust pie

1 large egg, beaten

Yield: 1 nine-inch pie

Preheat the oven to 400 degrees.

Mix the sugar, cornstarch, and cinnamon together in a small bowl. Place the cherries in a medium saucepan. Mix in the sugar mixture. Add the lemon juice and almond extract. Cook the mixture over medium heat, stirring constantly, till it begins to thicken. Boil it for about 1 minute more. The mixture is thickened properly when it coats the back of a spoon. Add the butter; stir till it is melted. Set it aside and let it cool.

Roll out the bottom piecrust and place it in the bottom of the pie pan. Brush the bottom of the piecrust with a lightly beaten egg. Spoon the filling into the crust. Roll out the top crust and cover the filling. Seal the edges and vent the top with a knife. Place the pie on a cookie sheet to catch any drips.

Bake the pie for 50 minutes or until the crust is brown and the filling is bubbly.

Homemade Mincemeat

A friend of mine gave me this recipe years ago and I have used it for Tate's Bake Shop pies ever since. I always thought I disliked mincemeat, but I really love this version. Baked in a pie, it may be served with fresh whipped cream or vanilla ice cream for a memorable holiday dessert.

❧

Coarsely chop the apricots, dates, and figs. Put them in a large bowl. Add the cranberries and both raisins and toss the ingredients.

Chop the apples and pears. Add them to the dried fruit mixture.

Stir in the melted shortening, brown sugar, lemon juice, and zest, apricot jam, all the spices, brandy, and sherry. Let the mixture macerate, covered, in the refrigerator, stirring every other day for one week.

NOTE: Mincemeat keeps all through the Thanksgiving and Christmas season so you only need to make it once for the holidays.

TO BAKE IN A PIE: Preheat the oven to 375 degrees.

Fill one buttermilk piecrust (recipe on page 73) with half the mincemeat recipe.

Place the pie on a cookie sheet to catch any drips.

Bake the pie for approximately 1 hour or until the crust is golden and the mincemeat bubbles slightly.

1/4 pound dried California apricots
1/4 pound dates, pitted
1/4 pound dried figs
1/4 pound dried cranberries
1/4 pound dark raisins
1/4 pound golden raisins
1/2 pound apples, peeled and cored
1/2 pound pears, peeled and cored
1/2 pound vegetable shortening or lard, melted
1 cup firmly packed dark or light brown sugar
1 lemon, grated zest and juice
1/4 cup apricot jam
1/2 teaspoon allspice
1/2 teaspoon cinnamon
1/4 teaspoon nutmeg
1/4 teaspoon cloves
1/4 teaspoon ginger
1/2 cup brandy
1/2 cup sherry

Yield: 2 quarts, or enough for two 9-inch pies

Orange Moss

My grandmother had a well-deserved reputation as a fine cook and baker. She used to make this light dessert often. Serve it as is or with shortbread cookies. This is definitely one of my childhood memory favorites.

❧

1 small package (3 ounces)
  lemon gelatin
2 cups boiling water
¼ cup sugar
1 teaspoon fresh lemon juice
1 orange, grated zest and
  juice
1 cup heavy cream

Yield: 8 servings

Dissolve the gelatin in the boiling water. Add the sugar, lemon juice, the juice from the orange, and the grated zest. Stir it until the ingredients are combined.

Chill the mixture until it is cold and syrupy, about one hour.

Whip the cream till it is thick. Fold it into the gelatin mixture and chill it for a few hours, or overnight.

You can either refrigerate the moss all in one bowl or divide it into separate serving dishes.

Fresh Blueberry and White Chocolate Tart

This blueberry tart is quick and simple to make. I love the whipped cream sweetened with white chocolate. I made this at a pie and tart class I was teaching at Loaves and Fishes Cook Shop in Bridgehampton, and I curdled the cream and chocolate in front of all my students! In the spirit of Julia Child, we just laughed and started over. Nothing is ever perfect!

In a small saucepan, mix ½ cup of the heavy cream with the white chocolate. Over low heat, mix until the chocolate is completely melted. Remove from heat. Add the remaining cream and stir until combined. Refrigerate the mixture till it's cold.

With an electric mixer, beat the white chocolate cream mixture till soft peaks form, just as you would in making whipped cream.

Spoon the mixture into the prepared tart shell. You can brush the bottom of the tart shell with chocolate (white or bittersweet) or with jam if you prefer.

Top the tart with fresh blueberries.

9-inch prebaked tart shell
(recipe on page 71)

½ cup white chocolate
1 cup heavy cream
4 cups fresh blueberries

Yield: 1 nine-inch tart

97

Apple Cranberry Crisp

Apple cranberry crisp is my favorite fall crisp. I taught my students this recipe at the Roger's Memorial Library in Southampton and it was a big hit. The cinnamon syrup drizzled over the ice cream or whipped cream really sets this crisp apart from the ordinary.

CRUMB TOPPING

½ cup all-purpose flour

¼ cup sugar

½ cup firmly packed dark or
  light brown sugar

2 teaspoons cinnamon

½ teaspoon nutmeg

7 tablespoons butter, cut
  into pieces

½ cup walnuts, chopped

FRUIT MIXTURE

4 cups apples, sliced and
  peeled

2 teaspoons cinnamon

1 ½ cups orange juice

¾ cup sugar

1 tablespoon orange zest

¼ teaspoon nutmeg

2 cups cranberries, fresh or
  frozen

Yield: 6 servings

Preheat the oven to 350 degrees. Grease an 8-inch square baking dish.

TO MAKE THE TOPPING: Mix the flour, sugars, cinnamon, and nutmeg in a medium bowl. Add the butter and mix it with your hands or a pastry blender until the mixture becomes crumbly. Add the walnuts and mix them in lightly. Set the topping aside.

TO MAKE THE FRUIT MIXTURE: In a large bowl, combine the apples and 1 teaspoon of the cinnamon. In a medium saucepan, combine the orange juice, sugar, orange zest, nutmeg, and the remaining teaspoon of the cinnamon. Bring the mixture to a boil, stirring until the sugar dissolves. Add the cranberries and cook them until they begin to pop, about 5 minutes. Strain the cranberries from the liquid and add them to the apple mixture and toss them together. Continue to boil the liquid mixture until it is reduced to 1 cup. Add ¾ cup of the resulting syrup to the apple cranberry mixture. Pour half of the apple mixture into the prepared baking dish. Sprinkle half of the crumb topping over the apple mixture. Top that with the remaining apple mixture, and top that apple mixture with the remaining crumb mixture. Reserve ¼ cup of the cinnamon syrup for drizzling over the crisp at the table.

Bake the crisp for 45 minutes or until it is bubbly and brown.

Blueberry Crisp

When my cycling friend Al Loreto turned fifty, he wanted blueberry crisp for forty people instead of a birthday cake. I have reduced the quantities to make a more manageable size, but this recipe does expand well if the opportunity arises.

Preheat the oven to 350 degrees.

TO MAKE THE BLUEBERRY MIXTURE: Combine 2 cups of blueberries and ¼ cup sugar in a medium saucepan. Cook the mixture over low heat. When the blueberries start to soften, stir in the cornstarch mixture and cook, stirring frequently, until the mixture thickens and clears. Stir in the remaining 3 cups of blueberries. Pour the mixture into an 8 × 8-inch square pan.

TO MAKE THE TOPPING: Mix the flour, walnuts, brown sugar, granulated sugar, and cinnamon in a medium bowl. Add the butter and mix it with your hands or a pastry cutter until the mixture forms moist crumbs. Sprinkle the crumb mixture on top of the blueberries.

Bake the crisp for 40 minutes or until the topping is golden and the filling is bubbling.

Cool slightly, and serve the crisp with whipped cream or ice cream.

BLUEBERRY MIXTURE

5 cups blueberries, fresh or frozen
¼ cup sugar
1 tablespoon cornstarch mixed with 2 tablespoons cold water or juice

CRUMB TOPPING

¾ cup plus 2 tablespoons all-purpose flour
½ cup chopped walnuts, toasted
3 tablespoons firmly packed dark or light brown sugar
3 tablespoons sugar
½ teaspoon cinnamon
6 tablespoons salted butter, chopped

Yield: 6 servings

CAKES

No Citron Fruit Cake

This cake is not the traditional style that usually ends up in the garbage after Christmas. It looks very natural and beautiful and can be made a month in advance to avoid the holiday frenzy. Sliced thin and served with cream cheese, it makes a great snack. It can also be serve with a cheese course and a dessert wine.

Preheat the oven to 300 degrees. Line a 10-inch tube pan with aluminum foil, pressing out any wrinkles so the cake surface will be smooth.

In a large bowl or pot, combine the dried fruits and the sherry. Let it stand for 45 minutes, stirring occasionally.

In another large bowl, stir together the flour, sugar, and baking powder.

Stir the mixed nuts and pecans into the fruit mixture. Remove 1½ cups and set it aside.

Stir the flour mixture into the fruit and nut mixture, making sure everything is well coated. Stir in the eggs and mix them well. Spoon the batter into the prepared pan. Pack it firmly to eliminate air pockets. Arrange the reserved 1½ cups of fruit and nut mixture on top.

Cover the pan loosely with aluminum foil and bake the cake for 2 hours. Remove the foil and bake it for another ½ hour or until a cake tester or toothpick inserted in the center comes out clean.

Remove the pan to a wire rack. Cool the cake for 30 minutes before peeling off the foil and removing the cake from the pan. Finish cooling the cake on the rack.

Wrap the fruitcake tightly with foil or plastic wrap. Store in the refrigerator or any cool place.

1 pound dried fruit: pears, apricots, peaches, pineapples, etc.

12 ounces dried pitted prunes

10 ounces dried pitted dates

4 ounces dried figs

½ cup cream sherry

1 ½ cups all-purpose flour

¾ cup sugar

1 teaspoon baking powder

2 12-ounce cans salted mixed nuts (no peanuts)

1 ½ cups pecans, halved or chopped

6 large eggs, lightly beaten

Yield: 1 ten-inch cake

Carrot Cake

In the seventies carrot cake became very popular because it was considered a healthy alternative to regular cakes. Sadly, this was not true, but it has maintained its popularity through the years. This cake is not delicate, and it is uncomplicated to make.

⚘

2 cups all-purpose flour
2 teaspoons baking powder
1 ½ teaspoons baking soda
1 teaspoon salt
2 teaspoons cinnamon
1 ¾ cups sugar
1 ½ cups vegetable oil
4 large eggs
2 cups grated carrots
½ cup chopped walnuts
1 cup crushed and drained
   pineapple

Cream Cheese Icing (recipe
   on page 105)

*Yield: 1 nine-inch two-layer
cake*

Preheat the oven to 350 degrees. Grease and flour, or line with waxed paper, two 9-inch round cake pans.

In a large bowl, stir together the flour, baking powder, baking soda, salt, and cinnamon.

In another large bowl, mix the sugar and oil. Beat in the eggs with an electric mixer. Stir in the carrots, nuts, and pineapple. Stir in the flour mixture. Pour the batter into the prepared pans.

Bake the cake for 45 minutes or until a cake tester or toothpick inserted into the center comes out clean. Remove the pans to a wire rack. Cool the cake for 15 minutes in the pans before removing them. Finish cooling the layers on the rack.

Spread the cream cheese icing between the 9-inch layers and on the sides and top of the cake.

Cream Cheese Icing

This icing is made for carrot cake, but I also love it on devil's food cake and hummingbird cake.

In a large bowl, cream together the cream cheese and butter with an electric mixer. Add the vanilla and mix it in. Beat in the sugar. Scrape down the sides of the bowl and beat the mixture again. Add the pineapple juice, if desired, and mix it well.

3 8-ounce packages of cream cheese, softened to room temperature

1/2 cup salted butter, softened to room temperature

2 teaspoons vanilla

2 1/2 cups confectioners' sugar

3 tablespoons pineapple juice (optional)

Yield: Enough icing for 2 nine-inch cake layers

Yellow Cake

This yellow cake is not too light, but it is very buttery and flavorful—just perfect for a simple old-fashioned cake that can be iced and filled with anything you desire. I love it with simple chocolate icing (recipe on page 107), but fresh fruit and whipped cream or cream cheese icing (recipe on page 105) and coconut would also be tempting.

2½ cups all-purpose flour

½ teaspoon baking soda

1 teaspoon baking powder

1 teaspoon salt

1 cup salted butter, softened
   to room temperature

2 cups sugar

4 large eggs, separated

1 teaspoon vanilla

1 cup sour cream

*Yield: 1 nine-inch two-layer
cake*

Preheat the oven to 350 degrees. Grease and flour or place waxed paper in the bottom of two 9-inch round cake pans.

In a large bowl, sift together the flour, baking soda, baking powder, and salt.

In another large bowl, cream the butter and sugar with an electric mixer until the mixture is light and fluffy. Add the egg yolks one at a time, mixing them in well after each addition. Beat in the vanilla. Add the dry ingredients alternately with the sour cream, ending with the dry ingredients.

In a separate bowl, beat the egg whites until they are stiff. Fold the egg whites into the cake batter and pour it into the prepared pans.

Bake the cake for 25 to 30 minutes or until a toothpick or cake tester inserted in the center comes out clean. Remove the pans to a wire rack. Cool the pans for 10 minutes before removing the cake from the pans. Finish cooling the cake on a rack.

Use your choice of icing or other topping (recipes on pages 105, 107, 113, 114, 116, and 118).

Chocolate Icing

This chocolate icing is very smooth and creamy, and is a tasty, all-around icing for yellow cake, chocolate cupcakes, or brownies.

❧

Melt the butter and the chocolate chips in the top of a double boiler. Stir in the milk. Add the vanilla. Stir in the confectioners' sugar until all of the ingredients are thoroughly mixed.

Chill the mixture for 45 minutes, then beat it with an electric mixer every 15 minutes (chilling the mixture between beatings) until it becomes light and thick enough to spread. (This will take 3 to 4 beatings.)

½ cup salted butter
1 ½ cups semisweet
   chocolate chips
⅔ cup milk
1 teaspoon vanilla
1 cup confectioners' sugar

Yield: 3 ½ cups, or enough to ice a 9-inch layer cake or 24 cupcakes.

Cheesecake

I know that there are many variations on cheesecake, and people either like them heavy or light. If you love the taste and texture of cream cheese, this one is for you.

❦

1 Graham Cracker Crust
(recipe on page 89)

4 8-ounce packages cream
cheese, softened to room
temperature
2 cups sugar
8 large eggs, separated
2 cups sour cream
2 tablespoons vanilla

Yield: 1 ten-inch cake

Prepare the graham cracker crust. Press it evenly into the bottom of a 10-inch springform pan. Refrigerate it till you are ready to use it.

Preheat the oven to 350 degrees.

In a large bowl, cream the cheese with an electric mixer. Add the sugar and mix it till it's creamy and smooth. Add the egg yolks one at a time. Scrape down the sides of the bowl and mix it again. Mix in the sour cream and vanilla.

In a separate bowl, beat the egg whites until they are stiff. Fold the egg whites into the cream cheese mixture. Pour the mixture into the crust. Wrap a piece of heavy-duty aluminum foil around the bottom and up the sides of the pan. Set the springform pan in a roasting pan half filled with boiling water. Place it in the oven.

Bake the cheesecake for 1 hour and 20 minutes or until the cake is golden brown and firm. If the top cracks, and the appearance bothers you, top the cake with fresh fruit.

Cool the cheesecake in the oven with the door half open for an hour, then remove it and refrigerate it overnight.

Chocolate Mousse Cake

Chocolate mousse cake is still one of the biggest sellers at Tate's Bake Shop. It can be made in advance and frozen without the whipped cream, making it ideal for impromptu entertaining. Everyone enjoys this cake—even people who don't love chocolate!

TO MAKE THE CRUST: Grind the chocolate wafers in a blender or food processor. Place them in a small bowl and add the melted butter. Press the crumb mixture into a 10-inch springform pan, covering the bottom and the sides evenly. Refrigerate the pan.

TO MAKE THE MOUSSE FILLING: Melt the chocolate in the top of a double boiler. Remove it from the heat and transfer the softened chocolate to a large bowl. Add the whole eggs and mix them in well, using an electric mixer. Add the egg yolks and mix it together. Scrape down the sides of the bowl and mix it again.

In a separate bowl, whip the heavy cream until soft peaks form.

In another bowl, beat the egg whites until they are stiff. Fold the cream and egg whites into the chocolate mixture until it is completely incorporated. Pour the mixture into the prepared crust and chill it overnight, or freeze it for future use.

TO MAKE THE TOPPING: Whip the heavy cream with the sugar and vanilla until stiff peaks begin to form.

Loosen the crust on all sides using a sharp knife and remove the sides of the springform pan. Cover the cake evenly with the cream topping 1 hour before serving.

CRUST

3 cups chocolate wafer crumbs
9 tablespoons salted butter, melted

MOUSSE FILLING

2¾ cups semisweet chocolate
2 large eggs
4 large eggs, separated
2 cups heavy cream

TOPPING

1½ cups heavy cream
2 tablespoons sugar
1 teaspoon vanilla

Yield: 1 ten-inch round cake or 2 seven-inch round cakes

Hummingbird Cake

My friend Hakan Cilingiroglu baked this old-style layer cake for my engagement party. Everyone loved it! The texture is similar to that of a carrot cake, but the flavors are banana and pineapple.

෨

3 cups all-purpose flour
1 teaspoon baking soda
1 teaspoon cinnamon
½ teaspoon salt
1¼ cups vegetable oil
1¾ cups sugar
3 large eggs
2 cups mashed very ripe
   bananas
1 8-ounce can crushed
   pineapple, drained
1 cup unsweetened
   desiccated coconut
   (Angel Flake is fine if you
   can't find this ingredient;
   it is just less sweet.)
¾ cup pecans, chopped
1 tablespoon vanilla

Yield: 1 nine-inch layer cake

Preheat the oven to 350 degrees. Grease two 9 × 2-inch round cake pans. Line the bottoms with waxed paper.

In a large bowl, mix the flour, baking soda, cinnamon, and salt.

In another large bowl, mix the oil and sugar. Add the eggs and mix them well. Scrape down the sides of the bowl. Stir in the bananas, pineapple, coconut, pecans, and vanilla. Stir in the flour mixture.

Spoon the mixture evenly between the prepared cake pans. The pans will be full, but don't worry about it: this batter doesn't rise much.

Bake the cake for 40 to 45 minutes or till a cake tester or toothpick inserted in the center comes out clean.

Cool the cake for 10 minutes in the pans and turn it out onto a wire rack to cool completely.

Ice it with cream cheese icing (recipe on page 105) or whipped cream (recipe on page 114) and refrigerate.

Devil's Food Cake

A moist, dark, and delicious layer cake, devil's food is one of our top selling cakes at Tate's Bake Shop. A versatile cake, it can be iced with cream cheese icing, chocolate icing, or peanut butter icing. You can also bake it in a 13 × 9-inch pan and serve it topped with whipped cream and fresh berries.

Preheat the oven to 350 degrees. Grease and flour or place waxed paper in the bottom of two 9-inch round pans or three 8-inch round pans.

In a large bowl, sift together the flour, baking soda, and salt.

In another large bowl, cream the butter and sugar with an electric mixer. Add the eggs one at a time, mixing them well after each addition. Stir in the melted chocolate.

Add the flour mixture and buttermilk alternately to the butter mixture in three stages. Add the boiling water and vanilla. Mix them well, but don't overmix. The mixture will be very thin, so don't be alarmed by its consistency. Pour the batter into the prepared pans.

Bake the cake for 30 minutes or until a cake tester or toothpick inserted in the center comes out clean. Remove the pans to a wire rack. Cool them for 5 to 10 minutes before removing the cake from the pans. Finish cooling the cake on the rack.

Frost the cake with the icing of your choice (recipes on pages, 105, 107, 113, 114, 116, and 118).

2 1/4 cups cake flour
2 teaspoons baking soda
1/2 teaspoon salt
1 cup salted butter
2 1/4 cups firmly packed dark brown sugar
3 large eggs
3 squares (3 ounces) unsweetened chocolate, melted
1/2 cup buttermilk
1 cup boiling water
2 teaspoons vanilla extract

Yield: 1 nine-inch two-layer cake or 1 eight-inch three-layer cake

111

Flourless Chocolate Cake

In the eighties, this flourless chocolate cake was the rage. I always felt it was too rich, but this version is very easy to make and not as rich and sweet. If you love whipped cream, fill the top with fresh whipped cream and garnish it with fresh raspberries and raspberry sauce (recipes on page 113 and 114). This cake also freezes well.

⁊

2 cups semisweet chocolate
  (I like to use Callebaut.)
1 cup sugar
1 teaspoon instant espresso
  powder
¾ cup boiling water
1 cup salted butter, softened
6 large eggs, at room
  temperature
1 tablespoon vanilla

Yield: 1 nine-inch cake

Preheat the oven to 350 degrees. Line the bottom of a 9 × 3-inch springform pan with pan spray and a waxed paper circle.

In a food processor fitted with a metal blade, process the chocolate, sugar, and espresso powder till finely ground.

With the motor still running, add the boiling water and mix till the chocolate is melted. Add the butter and process until it is incorporated into the mixture. Scrape down the sides of the bowl.

Add the eggs and vanilla. Process till smooth. Pour the mixture into the prepared pan.

Bake the cake for 40 minutes. The cake will be puffy, and the center will be barely set.

Loosen the sides, cool the cake, and refrigerate it for a minimum of 3 hours. The cake will sink in the middle, but that makes a great well to hold all the whipped cream!

Raspberry Sauce

This very simple raspberry sauce is an adornment to chocolate cakes and brownies or great when just splashed over ice cream and fruit. It can be made a day in advance.

In a blender or food processor, blend the raspberries and sugar till the liquid and the sugar is dissolved. Strain the mixture through a fine sieve. This process can be a bit tedious because of all the seeds. Stir in the liqueur.

2 cups frozen raspberries, thawed (I always use frozen for this because fresh doesn't make a big difference in this recipe and frozen are a lot less expensive.)
1/4 cup sugar
1 tablespoon Grand Marnier (optional)

Yield: 1 cup

113

Whipped Cream

I tasted "whipped cream" in a can recently and I suggest that everyone take five minutes to prepare real whipped cream from scratch.

2 cups heavy cream
1/4 cup sugar
2 teaspoons vanilla

Yield: 4 cups

Pour the cream into a medium bowl and use an electric mixer or a handheld mixer to whip it. Add the sugar and vanilla. Beat it till stiff peaks just begin to form. A lighter texture is better than one that is too stiff.

NOTE: When I need just a small bit of whipped cream, I use a handheld mixer and beat the cream right in the glass measuring cup. It's easy and there are no extra dishes to wash.

German Chocolate Cake

Three of my dearest friends request German chocolate cake for their birthdays every year. How lucky I am that all three birthdays fall within the same week! I just set up a little assembly line and within an hour or so I am finished!

Preheat the oven to 350 degrees. Grease and flour three 9-inch round cake pans.

In a small saucepan, melt the chocolate and cream of coconut together, stirring continually. After it is thoroughly mixed set it aside to cool.

Mix the flour, salt, and baking soda together and set it aside.

In a separate bowl, using an electric mixer, beat the butter and sugar till the mixture is light and fluffy. Add the egg yolks one at a time, beating well after each addition and scraping down the sides of the bowl. Beat in the vanilla extract. Stir in the melted chocolate mixture and mix until combined.

Add the dry ingredients alternately with the buttermilk to the chocolate mixture, ending with the dry ingredients.

In a separate bowl, beat the egg whites to a soft peak. Fold ¼ of the egg whites into the cake mixture. Fold in the remaining egg whites.

Divide the batter among the prepared pans.

Bake for 25 minutes or until the edges start to pull away from the sides and the center feels springy to the touch.

Cool for 10 minutes in the pan and turn it out onto a wire rack to cool.

Spread the frosting (recipe on page 116) evenly between the three layers. The sides do not get iced.

4 ounces Baker's German's Sweet Chocolate
½ cup canned cream of coconut (Coco Lopez)
2 cups all-purpose flour
¼ teaspoon salt
1 teaspoon baking soda
1 cup salted butter, softened to room temperature
1 ¼ cups sugar
4 large eggs, separated
2 teaspoons vanilla extract
1 cup buttermilk

Yield: 1 nine-inch layer cake

German Chocolate Cake Frosting

When my friend Jan Rose stayed with me while her house was being renovated, she discovered this icing in my refrigerator. I think it became her meal of choice during her stay!

&

I cup unsalted butter

2 cups evaporated milk

6 large egg yolks, lightly beaten

I cup firmly packed dark brown sugar

2 teaspoons vanilla

2 cups shredded coconut (sweetened or unsweetened)

2 cups pecans, toasted lightly

Yield: Enough icing to frost a nine-inch layer cake

In a small saucepan, stir together the butter, milk, egg yolks, and sugar.

Cook the ingredients over low heat, stirring constantly until the mixture thickens and is golden brown.

Remove it from the heat. Cool it completely.

Stir in the pecans and coconut.

If you make this icing in advance, store it in a plastic container with a lid and bring it to room temperature before icing the cake, or microwave it briefly to just soften it.

Chocolate Fudge Cupcakes

Laurie Perper is a peanut butter nut. To celebrate her birthday I made these cupcakes for our annual outing at my friend's lake house in Pennsylvania. The finished cupcakes are very chocolaty and rich. They would also be fun made as minicupcakes, in which case forget the icing and glaze them with chocolate (recipe on page 133).

Preheat the oven to 350 degrees. Line eight cups of a 3 × 1½-inch muffin tin with paper liners, or spray them with cooking spray.

Combine the butter and chocolate in a medium microwavable bowl. Microwave the mixture on low, stirring occasionally, till it is just melted. Stir in the sugars. Add the eggs, one at a time, mixing after each one. Stir in the vanilla, then the flour.

Divide the mixture into 8 muffin cups.

Bake the cupcakes for 20 to 25 minutes or until a cake tester or toothpick comes out with moist crumbs attached (similar to a brownie). Let them cool completely before icing them.

Ice with peanut butter icing (recipe on page 118).

6 tablespoons salted butter

6 ounces bittersweet or semisweet chocolate, chopped

½ cup firmly packed dark brown sugar

⅓ cup sugar

2 large eggs

1 teaspoon vanilla

½ cup all-purpose flour

Yield: 8 cupcakes or 24 minicupcakes

Peanut Butter Icing

You can use this icing on cupcakes, brownies, or layer cakes. The peanut butter flavor really stands out.

❧

¾ cup confectioners' sugar

¾ cup creamy peanut butter (Do not use old-fashioned or freshly ground.)

¼ cup salted butter, softened to room temperature

½ teaspoon vanilla

¼ cup heavy cream

Yield: 2 cups

Put the confectioners' sugar, peanut butter, butter, and vanilla in a small bowl. With an electric mixer, beat the ingredients until they are creamy.

Add the heavy cream and beat the mixture till it is soft and creamy.

Spread the icing over the top of the cupcakes. Top the icing with chopped peanuts or sprinkles if desired.

NOTE: If you make this icing in advance, store it in the refrigerator in a plastic container with a lid. Bring it to room temperature before icing the cupcakes.

Chocolate Chip Cake

A very simple, moist, sweet cake for picnics, breakfast, or church bake sales. There is no need for an icing, and it transports well.

Preheat the oven to 350 degrees. Grease a 13 × 9-inch pan. Set it aside.

In a medium bowl, combine the flour, baking powder, salt, and baking soda. Set it aside.

In a bowl with an electric mixer, cream the butter till it's light and creamy, about 4 minutes. Add the sugars and mix well. Add the vanilla and mix. Add the eggs, one at a time, mixing them well and scraping down the sides of the bowl after each addition.

Remove ¼ cup of the flour mixture and toss it with the chocolate chips in a separate bowl. This keeps the chips from sinking to the bottom of the cake. Set it aside.

Add the remaining flour mixture alternately with the sour cream in three stages, beginning and ending with the flour. Mix in the heavy cream. Stir in the chocolate chip mixture.

Spoon the batter into the prepared pan and spread it evenly.

Bake the cake for 55 minutes or until a cake tester or toothpick comes out clean.

3 cups all-purpose flour
1 teaspoon baking powder
1 teaspoon salt
¼ teaspoon baking soda
1 cup salted butter, softened to room temperature
¾ cup sugar
1¼ cups firmly packed light brown sugar
1 tablespoon vanilla
4 large eggs
2½ cups semisweet chocolate chips
1 cup sour cream
3 tablespoons heavy cream

Yield: 16 servings

Apple Cake

Apple cake is my husband's favorite. This one is very moist, with lots of apples and just the right touch of spice. Serve it for breakfast or as a dessert with vanilla ice cream or whipped cream.

&

2¼ cups sugar

2 teaspoons baking soda

1½ teaspoons cinnamon

1¼ teaspoons salt

3 large eggs

¾ cup vegetable oil

1½ teaspoons vanilla

8 cups apples, sliced into
¼-inch-thick slices
(I prefer Granny Smith),
peeled and cored

1½ cups walnuts, toasted
and chopped

3 cups all-purpose flour

Yield: 12 servings

Preheat the oven to 300 degrees.

Grease a 13 × 9 × 2-inch baking dish. Glass is best, but metal will be fine.

In a large bowl, mix the sugar, baking soda, cinnamon, and salt. Mix in the eggs, oil, and vanilla until the mixture is smooth.

Add the apples and walnuts, and stir till they are well coated.

Stir the flour in the mixture. (It will seem difficult in the beginning, but it will mix in.)

Bake the cake for 1 hour and 45 minutes. (Yes, this is the correct time.) Cool it completely in the baking dish. This cake keeps very well and is actually better the next day.

Warm Individual Chocolate Cakes

My mom and dad just celebrated their fifty-second wedding anniversary and I made this for their celebration because Mom is a chocolate lover. It is very easy to make, can be made a day in advance, and appears impressive to your guests—everything that makes a perfect dessert!

Preheat the oven to 450 degrees. Butter six ¾-cup ceramic ramekins (soufflé dishes).

Stir the chocolate and butter together in a medium saucepan over low heat. Stir in the vanilla. Cool the mixture slightly.

Whisk the eggs, yolks, and sugar together in a large bowl. Add the chocolate mixture and flour. Pour the mixture into the prepared dishes, dividing equally. Cover the ramekins and chill them if you are making this cake a day in advance; otherwise continue to the next step.

Bake the cakes until the sides are set but the center remains soft, about 11 to 15 minutes. (Use the longer oven time if you have refrigerated the batter.) You really do want the center soft so that it is runny on the inside, so remove the cakes from the oven promptly—and don't second-guess yourself.

Immediately, run a small knife around the edges to loosen the cakes. Turn the cakes out onto plates and serve them with your favorite ice cream or dessert sauce—or both!

6 ounces bittersweet
    chocolate, chopped
10 tablespoons salted butter
1 teaspoon vanilla
3 large eggs
3 large egg yolks
1 ¼ cups powdered sugar,
    sifted
½ cup all-purpose flour

Yield: 6 cakes

Raspberry Charlotte

My friend Tish Rehill begged me to make raspberry charlotte for the bake shop after I had made it at home for a party. I never added it to Tate's line, but when Tish turned fifty, I made sure that I surprised her with her favorite dessert. This takes a bit of time, but if you divide up the stages, it is manageable and well worth the effort.

SPONGE ROLL

1 cup all-purpose flour

1/4 teaspoon salt

6 large eggs, separated

1 1/4 cups sugar, divided

1 tablespoon vanilla

2 tablespoons salted butter, melted and cooled

1/4 cup confectioners' sugar, for dusting

1/2 cup raspberry jam

1 tablespoon raspberry liqueur (eau de framboise)

RASPBERRY SUGAR SYRUP

1/4 cup water

3 tablespoons sugar

1/4 cup raspberry liqueur (eau de framboise)

TO MAKE THE SPONGE ROLL: Preheat the oven to 350 degrees. Grease a 17 × 12-inch jelly roll pan and line the bottom with waxed paper.

In a small bowl, sift together the flour and salt. Set it aside.

In a large mixing bowl, beat the egg yolks, 3/4 cup of the sugar, and the vanilla with an electric mixer till it's very thick and pale yellow in color. Set it aside.

Place the egg whites in a large mixing bowl with the whisk attachment and beat them until soft peaks form. Slowly add the remaining 3/4 cup sugar and continue beating the whites until glossy stiff peaks form.

With a rubber spatula, fold a third of the egg whites into the yolk mixture. Fold in the remaining egg whites. Gently fold in the flour mixture, and then fold in the melted butter.

Spread the mixture into the prepared pan and spread it evenly.

Bake the sponge cake for 20 minutes or until the cake springs back when pressed with a fingertip.

Remove it from the oven and run a knife around the sides. Flip the sponge cake out onto a clean kitchen towel dusted with confectioners' sugar. Remove the waxed paper and cool the cake.

Invert a 1 1/2-quart bowl on one side of the sponge cake and cut a circle the size of the bowl with a sharp knife. Set the circle aside. Trim the remaining sponge cake into a rectangle so you can form it into a roll.

Mix the raspberry jam and the raspberry liqueur.

Spread the jam mixture over the sponge rectangle.

Starting from the longest side, roll the sponge tightly to from a log. Wrap it in clear plastic film. Tighten the ends, and freeze the log for a least an hour, or up to a few days if you are working in stages.

NOTE: The sponge roll makes a good simple dessert as is. Just slice it and serve.

TO MAKE THE RASPBERRY SYRUP: Place the water, sugar, and liqueur in a small saucepan. Heat the mixture over medium heat until the sugar dissolves. This only takes a minute or two. Set it aside to use on the mold.

TO MAKE THE TANGERINE BAVARIAN CREAM FILLING: Pour the tangerine juice into a small saucepan. Place it over medium heat and boil it until it is reduced to ¼ cup. This will take about 5 minutes or less. Cool the juice. Add the milk, orange peel, and vanilla bean. Bring the ingredients just to a boil. Set it aside for at least 20 minutes to infuse the flavors. (This mixture will curdle, but don't worry about that.)

In a medium bowl, whisk together the sugar, gelatin, and egg yolks.

Bring the milk mixture to just a boil again and whisk half the mixture slowly into the yolk mixture. Add the remaining hot-milk mixture and whisk.

Return the entire mixture to the stove and stir it constantly over medium heat until it begins to thicken. (Draw your finger across the back of the spoon; if it leaves a clear trail, the mixture is done.) Do not boil it or it will curdle, and curdling now *will* be a problem. Remove the saucepan from the heat and strain the custard into a clean bowl.

Cool the custard by placing the bowl in a larger bowl filled with ice. Stir occasionally for 15 minutes, or until the custard mixture begins to thicken around the edges.

Beat the heavy cream until it is thick. Fold it into the custard. Fold in the raspberries. Set it aside.

TANGERINE BAVARIAN CREAM FILLING

1 cup fresh-squeezed tangerine juice (about 3 large tangerines), or orange juice
1 ¾ cups milk
Peel of one orange, bitter white pith removed
1 vanilla bean, split lengthwise
½ cup sugar
1 tablespoon powdered gelatin
5 egg yolks

1 cup heavy cream
½ pint fresh raspberries

Yield: 12 servings

TO MAKE THE MOLD: Line the 1½-quart bowl with clear plastic wrap, keeping it as smooth as possible. Spray it lightly with cooking spray.

Remove the sponge roll from the freezer and trim the ends to neaten them. Cut the log into ¼-inch slices. Place 1 slice in the bottom of the bowl. Work your way up the sides with the remaining slices, fitting them tightly together. You may have to cut smaller pieces at the top for a tight fit. Basically, line the inside of the bowl so that it has a sponge cake lining.

Brush the sponge cake with the simple raspberry syrup, reserving a bit for the remaining large circle.

Pour the finished tangerine cream into the prepared mold. Place the reserved cake circle on top to fit snugly and brush it with the remaining syrup.

Wrap it in clear plastic wrap and put it in the refrigerator for at least 8 hours or up to two days before serving.

TO SERVE THE CHARLOTTE: Remove the charlotte from the refrigerator. Remove the top piece of clear film and invert the charlotte onto a serving platter. Remove the bowl. Remove the remaining clear film. Decorate the mold with whipped cream piped around the edges or with fresh raspberries.

Gingerbread

After years of searching for a gingerbread that reminded me of one I had in England when I was a college exchange student, I finally developed one, more than twenty years later! This cake is very moist and spicy and can be served many ways—plain, with whipped cream (recipe on page 114) and lemon curd (recipe page 82) folded in, or with ice cream—the variations are endless and fabulous! My Mom loves this cake just as it is.

Preheat the oven to 350 degrees.

Grease a 9 × 13-inch pan or two 9-inch round cake layer pans if you want to make a layer cake. I prefer the high squares that you can cut from a 9 × 13-inch pan. If you are using layer pans, always line the bottom of the pan with waxed paper and pan spray.

Put hot water into a measuring cup to warm it; pour it out before measuring the molasses. It keeps the molasses from sticking; this way it won't be such a mess. Melt the butter and molasses together.

In a small bowl, sift together the flour, baking soda, salt, ginger, cinnamon, nutmeg, and cloves. Set it aside.

In a large mixing bowl, using an electric mixer, beat the sugar and egg together till they are thick. Add the butter mixture and beat till it's combined. Add the flour mixture and beat till it's combined. Scrape down the sides of the bowl. Add the yogurt and orange zest and mix them in. Add the boiling water and beat it in for 2 minutes.

Pour the batter into the prepared pan.

Bake the gingerbread for 1 hour and 10 minutes or until a cake tester or toothpick inserted in the center comes out clean.

Remove the gingerbread from the oven and cool it in pans completely.

This cake freezes well and keeps for a few days at room temperature. It keeps even longer in the refrigerator if it is wrapped tight in clear plastic film or aluminum foil.

1 cup butter
1 cup dark unsulfured molasses
2 1/3 cups all-purpose flour
1 teaspoon baking soda
1/4 teaspoon salt
1 teaspoon ginger
1/2 teaspoon cinnamon
1/4 teaspoon nutmeg
1/8 teaspoon cloves
1 cup firmly packed dark brown sugar
1 large egg
2/3 cup plain yogurt, low fat or regular
1 tablespoon grated orange zest, from one orange
3/4 cup boiling water

Yield: 12 servings

Almond Butter Cake

This is my friend Veronica Higgins's favorite cake. I made this once for her birthday and she didn't believe that I took the time at home to bake for her. We still laugh about it. This cake is dense and moist and makes a great traditional wedding cake or birthday cake. You can finish this cake many different ways, but my favorite is with white chocolate butter-cream icing and raspberry filling.

1 cup cake flour

1 ½ teaspoons baking powder

½ cup salted butter, softened to room temperature

¾ cup sugar

1 11-ounce package almond paste

6 large eggs, room temperature

1 tablespoon vanilla

1 cup blanched slivered almonds, finely ground

Yield: 1 ten-inch layer cake

Preheat the oven to 325 degrees.

Prepare one 10-inch layer cake pan or springform pan with non-stick pan spray and waxed paper.

Sift the flour and baking powder into a small bowl. Set it aside.

Cream the butter and sugar with an electric mixer until they are well blended. Beat in the almond paste a few pieces at a time until the batter becomes a smooth paste. Add the eggs one at a time, beating well after each addition.

Add the vanilla and beat it in for 5 minutes.

Mix in the ground almonds and dry ingredients until they are just combined.

Spoon the batter into the prepared pan and smooth the top.

Bake the cake for 60 minutes or until a cake tester or toothpick inserted in the middle comes out clean.

Slice the cake horizontally into three layers and fill with raspberry blueberry filling (recipe on page 127) and ice with cream cheese icing (recipe on page 105).

Raspberry Blueberry Filling

This filling is very quick to make and not too rich. It complements an almond cake, yellow cake, or chocolate cake. Leftover filling may be swirled into plain yogurt for a breakfast treat.

In a small saucepan, put the blueberries, raspberries, and sugar. Over low heat, stir them until the berries start to soften. Simmer for about 10 minutes, or until the mixture thickens slightly. Let it cool completely.

Spread the mixture evenly between the cake layers. If you are baking the almond cake, cut the 10-inch cake into three layers. Fill the cake with berry filling, top with another cake layer, and repeat.

Frost the cake with your favorite icing.

2½ cups blueberries, fresh or frozen
2½ cups raspberries, fresh or frozen
⅓ cup sugar

Yield: 2½ cups

Sour Cream Coffee Cake

My husband ate this cake every weekend for a year before he actually met me. He claims that, now that he knows the baker, he hasn't seen the cake since! Everyone always loves this coffee cake. It is moist and very rich and can keep for several days. Served warm, this cake is outstanding.

❧

½ cup sugar

2 cups pecans, chopped

1 tablespoon cinnamon

1 cup salted butter

1½ cups sugar

2 eggs

2 cups sour cream

1 tablespoon vanilla

2 cups all-purpose flour

1 tablespoon baking powder

¼ teaspoon salt

Yield: 1 ten-inch cake

Preheat the oven to 350 degrees. Grease and flour a 10-inch Bundt pan.

In a small bowl, combine the ½ cup sugar, pecans, and cinnamon. Set it aside.

Cream the butter and 1½ cups of sugar till they are light and fluffy. Add the eggs, mixing well. Add the sour cream and vanilla.

Sift the flour, baking powder, and salt into a small bowl.

Fold the dry ingredients into the butter mixture.

Pour half of the cake mixture into the prepared pan. Sprinkle the batter with half of the pecan mixture. Add the remaining cake batter and spread it evenly over the top of the pecan mixture. Sprinkle the remaining pecan mixture evenly over the top of the cake.

Bake the cake for 1 hour and 10 minutes or until a cake tester or toothpick inserted in the center comes out clean.

Lime Mousse Cake

I am not a big cheesecake lover anymore, but I love both key lime pie and mousse cake. Lime mousse cake is like having all the things I love in one cake.

❧

TO MAKE THE CRUST: Combine the sugar cookie crumbs, ginger, and melted butter. Press the mixture into a 10-inch springform pan.

TO MAKE THE FILLING: Sprinkle the gelatin over the lime juice. Set it aside to soften.

Bring ½ cup of the heavy cream to a simmer in a small saucepan. Turn off the heat and add the white chocolate. Stir till it is smooth. (This mixture stiffens up quickly, but will smooth out.) Set it aside.

In a large bowl, using an electric mixer, mix the cream cheese, sugar, and lime zest till they are smooth. Add the white chocolate mixture to the cream cheese mixture and blend it well. Add the gelatin mixture and blend thoroughly.

In a separate bowl, whip the cream till it is thick. Fold it into the cream cheese mixture.

Spoon the mixture into the prepared pan. Refrigerate it overnight. You can make this in the morning and serve it at night if you didn't plan in advance.

CRUST

2 cups sugar cookies, ground fine in a food processor (You can also use graham crackers.)

¼ cup crystallized ginger, chopped fine

4 tablespoons salted butter, melted

FILLING

1 envelope gelatin (2 teaspoons)

⅔ cup fresh lime juice, about 6 limes

2½ cups heavy cream

9 ounces white chocolate or 1½ cups chopped

3 8-ounce packages of cream cheese, softened to room temperature

1 cup, 2 tablespoons sugar

1 tablespoon grated lime zest from one lime

Yield: 1 ten-inch cake

Chocolate Hazelnut Fudge Cake

I made this for my niece Christina, a real chocolate lover, for her twenty-second birthday. This impressive cake is easy to make, and can be baked a couple of days in advance. Serve it as is, or cover it with a chocolate glaze (recipe on page 133) or with whipped cream and berries.

10 ounces bittersweet
　chocolate
6 ounces milk chocolate
1 cup Nutella
½ cup praline paste
6 large eggs
¼ cup sugar
1 cup heavy cream
1 teaspoon vanilla

Yield: 12 to 14 servings

Preheat the oven to 350 degrees.

Butter or spray a 10-inch springform pan. Wrap the bottom and sides with heavy-duty aluminum foil to waterproof the pan for the water bath.

Melt the chocolates in the top of a double boiler or a microwave, stirring the mixture till it's smooth. Remove it from the heat and stir in the Nutella and praline paste.

In a large bowl, beat the eggs and sugar with an electric mixer till they are pale and thick. Add the chocolate mixture and mix them well.

In a separate bowl, add the vanilla to the cream and whip the cream till it holds soft peaks. Fold the whipped cream into the chocolate batter.

Pour the batter into the prepared springform pan and put it in a roasting pan. Add enough water to fill halfway up the side of the springform pan.

Bake the cake for 1 hour and 10 minutes. Turn off the oven and leave the cake inside for an additional 45 minutes. Remove the springform pan from the roasting pan and place it on a rack till it's completely cool.

Cranberry Crumb Cake

Sweet crisp crumbs, soft moist cake, and tart fresh cranberries—all my favorite flavors and textures in one bite of cranberry crumb cake. That is when I am not longing for chocolate!

❧

Preheat the oven to 350 degrees. Grease a 9-inch square pan with pan spray or butter.

TO MAKE THE TOPPING: In a medium bowl, combine the brown sugar, flour, cinnamon, and butter. Mix it with your fingertips or a pastry blender till the mixture resembles coarse crumbs. Add the walnuts and toss them together. Set the mixture aside in the refrigerator. (This can be done the night before.)

TO MAKE THE BATTER: In a medium bowl, combine the flour, ½ cup of the sugar, baking powder, cinnamon, and salt.

In a large bowl, beat the sour cream, eggs, oil, orange zest, and vanilla till combined.

In a small bowl, toss the cranberries with 2 tablespoons of sugar and set the mixture aside.

Add the flour mixture to the sour cream mixture and stir till they are combined. Fold in the cranberries.

Spoon the batter into the prepared pan. Sprinkle the topping evenly over the batter.

Bake the cake for 45 minutes or until a cake tester or toothpick comes out clean.

TOPPING

½ cup firmly packed dark or light brown sugar

½ cup all-purpose flour

½ teaspoon cinnamon

5 tablespoons salted butter, cut into tablespoons

½ cup coarsely chopped walnuts

BATTER

2 cups all-purpose flour

½ cup plus 2 tablespoons sugar

2 teaspoons baking powder

¼ teaspoon cinnamon

¼ teaspoon salt

⅔ cup sour cream

2 large eggs

¼ cup walnut oil (You can use vegetable oil if that is all you have.)

1 teaspoon grated zest, from one orange

1 teaspoon vanilla

1 ½ cups cranberries, coarsely chopped (frozen is fine)

Yield: 12 servings

Bob's Mud Cake

Bob Sielaff, my professor at Cobleskill College, gave me this recipe years ago. I never got around to making it until I started working on this book. When I first tried it, warm from the oven, I thought, "I don't get it. It's not so great." I put the cake in the refrigerator and went to bed thinking Bob must be nuts. In the morning, I tried it again, just to make sure. I was shocked to find that it was marvelous. I think this cake must be served cold, but make it and decide for yourself.

2 cups all-purpose flour

1 teaspoon baking soda

1¾ cups strong brewed
   coffee

¼ cup bourbon

5 ounces unsweetened
   chocolate

1 cup salted butter

2 cups sugar

2 large eggs

1 teaspoon vanilla

Yield: 12 servings

Preheat the oven to 275 degrees. Butter or spray a 10-inch Bundt pan and sift unsweetened cocoa powder in it to completely dust the pan.

In a medium bowl, mix the flour and baking soda. Set it aside.

In a medium saucepan, mix the coffee, bourbon, chocolate, and butter over low heat. Stir the ingredients until the butter and chocolate are melted. Pour the mixture into a large bowl and beat it with an electric mixer.

Add the sugar, a little at a time. Beat it in until the sugar is dissolved. Add the flour mixture, a little at a time, to make the batter.

Beat in the eggs and vanilla until the batter is smooth. (This mixing method is untraditional, but it works.)

Pour the batter into the prepared pan and bake it for 1 hour and 15 minutes or until a cake tester or toothpick comes out clean when inserted into the center.

Cool the cake completely before turning it onto a plate.

Refrigerate the cake and serve it with whipped cream (recipe on page 114) or ice cream, or you can make a chocolate water glaze (recipe on page 133) to pour over the outside and sprinkle it with chopped pecans.

Chocolate Water Glaze

Melt the chocolate in the top of a double boiler. Add the water slowly, using a wire whisk. The mixture will stiffen up at first, but keep adding the water and it will thin out to a nice pouring consistency.

Place the cake on a wire rack and pour the glaze slowly over the cake, covering it completely. Sprinkle nuts on the top while the glaze is still wet.

Refrigerate the cake till you are ready to serve it.

8 ounces semisweet
   chocolate
1/4 cup or more of warm
   water.

*Yield: enough glaze for 1
ten-inch Bundt cake*

Tres Leches Cake

My Latin American staff taught me the recipe for this delicious cake. Tres Leches is a very popular cake in Mexico. When they first told me about it, I thought it sounded odd, but curiosity made me try it. It is fabulous and tastes like the best strawberry whipped cream cake you will ever have. It is a bit messy to put together, but worth it.

౸

CAKE

9 large eggs, room temperature

2 cups all-purpose flour

1 1/2 teaspoons baking powder

1 cup milk

1 teaspoon vanilla

3/4 cup salted butter, softened to room temperature

1 1/2 cups sugar

1/2 teaspoon cream of tartar

TO MAKE THE CAKE: Preheat the oven to 350 degrees. Line an 17 1/2 × 11 1/2-inch pan with waxed paper.

Separate the eggs, putting the egg yolks in a small bowl and the egg whites in a large bowl.

In a small bowl, combine the flour and baking powder.

Measure out the milk in a measuring cup and add the vanilla to it. Set it aside.

In another bowl cream the butter and sugar with an electric mixer till the mixture is pale yellow and fluffy, about 3 minutes.

Add the egg yolks and beat the mixture until it is fluffy again, about another 3 minutes. Make sure you scrape the bowl and beat it for another few seconds.

Alternately, in three stages, add the flour mixture and the milk mixture, starting and ending with the flour. Beat it until it is smooth after each addition and scrape down the sides of the bowl between additions.

Beat the egg whites with the cream of tartar until soft peaks form. Fold the egg whites into the butter mixture.

Pour the batter into the prepared pan.

Bake the cake for 20 minutes or until a cake tester or toothpick comes out clean and the center of the cake springs back when touched.

TO MAKE THE TRES LECHES: While the cake is baking, combine in a large bowl the heavy cream, evaporated milk, and sweetened condensed milk. Mix till they are combined.

When the cake is removed from the oven, let it cool 10 minutes in the pan.

Loosen the edges of the cake with a table knife and turn it over onto another sheet pan. You may have to poke holes in the cake with a fork or toothpick to facilitate soaking. Pour the milk mixture evenly over the top of the cake; this has to be done gradually, in stages, so that the cake can absorb all of the liquid. The sheet pan will catch the drippings, and you can later spoon any excess milk mixture back on top of the cake.

Refrigerate the cake overnight in the sheet pan.

TO MAKE THE ICING: Whip the heavy cream, sugar, and vanilla till it's just stiff.

TO ASSEMBLE THE CAKE: Remove the cake from the refrigerator and cut it in half down the middle, making two equal layers. Place one layer on a platter. Spoon part of the whipped cream over the cake. Add a layer of fresh strawberries or peaches and cover them with a thin coating of whipped cream.

Place the second cake layer on top of the strawberries or peaches.

Ice the cake with the remaining whipped cream around the sides and top, covering the cake completely. Top with sliced fresh strawberries or peaches.

Refrigerate the cake till it's served.

TRES LECHES (THE THREE MILKS)

2 cups heavy cream
1 5-ounce can evaporated milk
1 14-ounce can sweetened condensed milk

WHIPPED CREAM ICING

2 cups heavy cream
2 tablespoons sugar
1 teaspoon vanilla

2 cups sliced fresh strawberries or peaches

Yield: 12 servings

Blueberry Buckle

Two of my good customers used this recipe to win a blueberry buckle bake-off in Maine. My niece Kara informed me that I needed to adjust the crumb topping because mine didn't hold its crumbly texture well. The recipe won without the adjustment, but I agree with my niece, so I added a little more flour to the crumb topping, making it an even better buckle!

CAKE BATTER

½ cup salted butter, softened to room temperature

¾ cup sugar

1 large egg

½ cup milk

2 teaspoons baking powder

½ teaspoon salt

2 cups all-purpose flour

2½ cups blueberries, fresh or frozen

TOPPING

1 cup firmly packed dark or light brown sugar

1 cup all-purpose flour

1 teaspoon cinnamon

½ cup salted butter, chilled

Yield: 1 nine-inch square buckle

Preheat the oven to 375 degrees. Grease a 9-inch-square pan.

In a large bowl, cream the butter and sugar until they are well combined. Add the egg, milk, baking powder, and salt. Mix the ingredients well. Stir in the flour 1 cup at a time, scraping down the sides of the bowl between additions. Fold in the blueberries. Spoon the batter into the prepared pan and set it aside.

TO MAKE THE TOPPING: Combine all the ingredients in a medium-sized bowl. Mix them with a pastry blender or your hands until they are combined and crumbly. Sprinkle it evenly on top of the cake batter.

Bake the cake for 45 to 50 minutes or until a cake tester or toothpick inserted in the center comes out clean.

Sticky Toffee Date Pudding

All my friends couldn't stop talking about a dessert from the Laundry Restaurant in East Hampton, so I had to go to try it. They were right. Sticky toffee date pudding is a wonderful, homey, sweet, gooey cake that would be a treat on a cold night. I hope you enjoy my rendition of this old English classic.

Preheat the oven to 350 degrees. Grease a 9-inch springform pan.

TO MAKE THE CAKE: Combine the dates and water in a small saucepan. Bring the mixture to a boil and simmer it for a minute. Remove it from the heat and add the baking soda. The mixture will bubble, but don't worry. Set it aside to cool.

In a small bowl, mix the flour and salt.

In a large bowl, cream the butter and sugar. Add the eggs and vanilla. Scrape down the sides of the bowl and mix it again. Add the date mixture and mix it well. Scrape down the sides of the bowl again. Add the flour mixture and blend it in. Add the baking powder and mix it again.

Pour the batter into the prepared pan. Wrap the bottom of the springform pan with aluminum foil and place the springform pan in a water bath that comes only halfway up the side of the pan.

Bake the cake for 45 to 50 minutes or until a cake tester or toothpick is inserted and comes out clean.

TO MAKE THE SAUCE: Combine the butter, sugar, heavy cream, and vanilla in a small saucepan. Bring the mixture to a boil, stirring occasionally. Remove it from the heat.

When the cake is removed from the oven, and while it is still hot, poke holes in it with a toothpick.

Pour the sauce slowly over the cake until all the sauce has seeped into the cake.

Serve it warm with ice cream or whipped cream.

CAKE BATTER

2 cups dates, pitted and chopped (8 ounces)

1 3/4 cups water

1 teaspoon baking soda

1 1/4 cups all-purpose flour

1/4 teaspoon salt

1/2 cup salted butter

1/2 cup firmly packed dark or light brown sugar

2 large eggs

1 teaspoon vanilla

2 teaspoons baking powder

SAUCE

1/2 cup salted butter

1/2 cup firmly packed dark or light brown sugar

1/2 cup heavy cream

1/2 teaspoon vanilla

Yield: 1 nine-inch cake

Coconut Birthday Cake

Every year I get together with my friend Bernie McCoy to celebrate her birthday. We always start the day off cycling, then pack a lunch for the beach, and end the day with her favorite cake. This coconut birthday cake is a very tall three-layer cake and versatile enough that you can change the filling or icing to suit your taste.

⌙

2¾ cups all-purpose flour
1 teaspoon baking powder
½ teaspoon baking soda
½ teaspoon salt
1½ cups sugar
1 cup salted butter, softened to room temperature
1 cup canned cream of coconut (Coco Lopez)
5 large eggs, separated
2 teaspoons vanilla
1 cup buttermilk
2 cups coconut flakes

Yield: 1 nine-inch three-layer cake

Preheat the oven to 350 degrees.

Prepare three 8-inch layer-cake pans with pan spray, and line the bottoms with waxed paper.

In a small bowl, combine the flour, baking powder, baking soda, and salt.

With an electric mixer, beat the sugar and butter till it's light and fluffy. Add the cream of coconut and beat it till it's fluffy. Beat in the egg yolks one at a time. Add the vanilla. Scrape down the sides of the bowl and mix it again.

Add the dry ingredients and mix till they are just combined. Add the buttermilk and mix it till it is combined.

In a separate mixing bowl, beat the egg whites until they are stiff, but not dry. Fold the egg whites into the batter.

Divide the batter evenly between the prepared pans.

Bake the cake for 40 to 45 minutes or until a cake tester or toothpick inserted into the center comes out clean.

Let the cake cool for 10 minutes in the pans and turn it out onto a wire rack to cool completely.

I like to ice this cake with cream cheese icing (recipe on page 105) and finish it with coconut flakes all over the top and sides.

Nanny Ethel's Kugel

My friend Sam Eber has raved about his family's kugel for years. He was very kind to make it for me and give me the recipe so that all of you can enjoy it, too. This is very rich and delicious. It can be frozen and reheated.

Preheat the oven to 400 degrees. Grease a 9-inch square Pyrex dish or similar casserole.

Cook the noodles in boiling water for 1 to 2 minutes and drain. Mix the butter, cream cheese, vanilla, sour cream, eggs, sugar, and milk until they are all well blended. Add the noodles and mix them in well.

Pour the mixture into the prepared pan. Turn the oven down to 325 degrees and bake the kugel for 1 to 1½ hours, depending on the depth of your pan. Kugel should be golden on the sides, and the center should not appear wet.

Serve it warm.

½ pound fine egg noodles
1 cup salted butter, melted
6 ounces cream cheese
1 teaspoon vanilla
1 cup sour cream
3 large eggs
½ cup sugar
2 cups milk

Yield: 8 servings

HEALTHY
ALTERNATIVES

Energy Bars

After years of cycling, I just couldn't bear to eat another commercial energy bar. Energy bars are quick to make and freeze well, plus they are durable enough to survive in a back pocket during a long ride or hike.

Preheat the oven to 350 degrees. Spray an 8-inch square baking pan with nonstick spray.

Mix the cereal, almonds, and fruits.

Combine the peanut butter and rice syrup in a small saucepan (to avoid a sticky mess, wet the inside of the measuring cup with warm water before measuring). Bring the peanut butter mixture to a boil and stir constantly for 30 seconds. Pour the mixture over the cereal mixture. Stir to combine them.

Place the mixture into the prepared pan. Wet your hands and press the mixture evenly and firmly into the pan.

Bake the mixture for 10 minutes.

Cool it completely. Loosen the edges with a table knife and flip the pan over onto a cutting board.

Cut it into squares. Wrap them individually and freeze them for your next adventure.

3 cups Kashi brand puffed whole grain cereal
1/2 cup almonds, chopped
1/4 cup dates, pitted and chopped (Spray the knife with cooking spray to make the chopping easier.)
1/4 cup dried cranberries
1/4 cup raisins
1/2 cup creamy peanut butter
1/2 cup brown rice syrup (available at most health food stores)

Yield: 12 squares

Whole Wheat Quick Bread

I love whole wheat low-sugar baked goods—this may be hard to believe because I am also a white flour and sugar junkie! This quick bread tastes very hearty toasted with butter, served plain, or with your favorite peanut butter or almond butter.

ॐ

1 cup wheat bran
½ cup wheat germ
2½ cups whole wheat flour
1 teaspoon salt
1½ teaspoons baking soda
2 cups buttermilk
½ cup molasses
½ cup raisins (optional)

Yield: 1 nine-inch loaf

Preheat the oven to 350 degrees. Spray a 9 × 5 × 3-inch loaf pan with nonstick cooking spray.

In a medium bowl, combine the wheat bran, wheat germ, flour, salt, and baking soda. In another bowl, mix the buttermilk and molasses.

Stir the buttermilk mixture into the flour mixture. Mix them well and fold in the raisins, if desired. Spoon the batter into the prepared loaf pan and spread it evenly. The mixture will look a little airy, but this is OK.

Bake the bread for 1 hour or until it is golden brown and firm on top.

Remove the bread from the oven and turn it over onto a wire rack. Turn it back over and cool it completely. After about 15 minutes, you can cut this warm loaf and spread it with butter, or slice it and freeze it so that you can toast it all week for your breakfast.

Healthy Pumpkin Bread

This pumpkin bread is a heavy, healthy bread that is low in fat and cholesterol. After tasting it you would never know that there is only one tablespoon of butter in it!

Preheat the oven to 350 degrees. Grease a 9 × 5 × 3-inch loaf pan.

Combine the flours, wheat germ, sucanat, salt, baking soda, baking powder, cardamom, nutmeg, cinnamon, and pecans. Stir the mixture and set it aside.

Combine the melted butter, pumpkin puree, rice syrup, and maple syrup in a medium bowl.

Beat the egg whites till they are stiff, but not dry. Fold them into the pumpkin mixture.

Fold the pumpkin and egg mixture into the flour mixture.

Spoon the batter into the prepared pan.

Bake the bread for 55 minutes or until it's firm to the touch and a cake tester or toothpick comes out clean when inserted into the middle of the loaf.

This bread will not rise and will be heavy, but the density works because the loaf can be sliced very thin.

½ cup whole wheat flour
½ cup unbleached all-purpose flour
½ cup oat flour
½ cup wheat germ
½ cup sucanat (granulated cane sugar), or raw sugar (available at most health food stores)
¼ teaspoon salt
¼ teaspoon baking soda
½ teaspoon baking powder
¼ teaspoon cardamom
¼ teaspoon nutmeg
½ teaspoon cinnamon
½ cup pecans, chopped
1 tablespoon salted butter, melted
¾ cup canned pumpkin puree
¼ cup brown rice syrup (available at most health food stores)
¼ cup pure maple syrup
4 large egg whites

Yield: 1 nine-inch loaf

Sunflower Whole Wheat Quick Bread

This very simple quick bread is delicious with soups or an easy Sunday supper. This bread complements assorted cheeses at dinner or butter and jam for breakfast.

2 cups stone-ground whole wheat flour

1 ½ cups unbleached all-purpose flour

½ cup wheat germ

¼ cup sugar

¼ cup firmly packed dark or light brown sugar

1 teaspoon salt

4 teaspoons baking powder

1 teaspoon baking soda

1 cup roasted sunflower seeds, unsalted

1 ½ cups buttermilk

2 large eggs

4 tablespoons salted butter, melted

Yield: 1 nine-inch loaf

Preheat the oven to 375 degrees. Grease a 9 × 5 × 3-inch loaf pan.

Combine the flours, wheat germ, sugars, salt, baking powder, and baking soda.

Stir in the sunflower seeds.

In a small bowl combine the buttermilk, eggs, and melted butter, and beat them until they are combined.

Add the buttermilk mixture to the flour mixture and stir them till they are just combined.

Spoon the batter into the prepared loaf pan.

Bake the bread for 50 to 60 minutes or until the loaf is brown and hollow sounding when tapped.

My Favorite Oatmeal Cereal

I love to prepare brunch with an assortment of sweets and eggs and a healthy alternative. This oatmeal is always a hit, even with the egg-and-buttered-toast people. This mixed grain oatmeal cereal may be eaten plain or with maple syrup and soy milk.

Preheat the oven to 350 degrees.

In a large, shallow, 2½-quart ovenproof dish, mix the grains, raisins, cranberries, butter, salt, and cinnamon. Add the water.

Stir all the ingredients together. Cover the dish loosely with aluminum foil and bake it for 1½ hours or until the grains are tender and the water is absorbed. Stir it every half hour. Be careful of the steam when you lift the foil.

⅓ cup barley
⅓ cup steel-cut oats (Irish oatmeal)
⅓ cup wheat berries
½ cup raisins
½ cup dried cranberries
2 tablespoons salted butter
½ teaspoon salt
1 teaspoon cinnamon
6 cups water (or 4 cups water and 2 cups soy milk)

Yield: 8 servings

Rena's Sport Bars

My six A.M. biking partner has the purest diet I have ever seen. She would never eat a commercial power bar, so she developed her own. I found that if I left my Cliff Bars at home, she would always share hers. Now I make my own, too. You can freeze them in individual bars and grab one in the morning for a booster two hours into your ride, or drive, or work, or just for a nutritious healthy snack anytime.

⅔ cup apple butter
⅔ cup natural peanut butter
¼ cup sesame seeds
¼ cup flax meal
2 cups rolled oats
½ cup dried cranberries

Yield: 12 bars

Preheat the oven to 300 degrees.

In a large bowl, combine the apple butter and peanut butter. Add the sesame seeds and flax meal. Mix them until they are combined. Add the oatmeal and cranberries. The mixture will be very stiff.

Place the mixture into an ungreased 8-inch square pan. Wet your hands and pat it evenly into the pan.

Bake it for 40 minutes or until it is golden brown and firm.

Cut it into bars while it's still warm.

Oatmeal Tahini Cookies

Oatmeal tahini cookies make a quick breakfast or afternoon snack. The taste reminds me of a less sweet Middle Eastern halvah.

Preheat the oven to 350 degrees. Grease two cookie sheets.

In a medium bowl, combine the tahini, honey, and cinnamon. Add the oatmeal, sesame seeds, and apple. I find it easier to mix this dough with my hands until it is thoroughly combined.

Using two tablespoons, drop the cookies 2 inches apart on the prepared cookie sheets. Pat down each cookie with your fingertips before baking it. They don't spread much.

Bake them for 15 minutes or until the edges begin to brown.

Cool the cookies on the baking sheet for 5 minutes and remove them to a wire rack to cool completely.

6 tablespoons tahini
1/3 cup honey
1/2 teaspoon cinnamon
1 1/2 cups instant quick oats
1/4 cup sesame seeds
3/4 cup apple, peeled, cored, and shredded

Yield: 16 cookies

Healthy Bran Muffins

Every Christmas I host a brunch for friends who may be alone that year. I have an eclectic group, so I always make sure I have both healthy and decadent items to choose from. These muffins are fine plain, but I also love them with natural peanut butter. They will probably not be a kid's favorite.

&

1 cup unprocessed wheat bran

⅔ cup whole wheat pastry flour

⅔ cup whole wheat flour

1¼ teaspoons baking soda

⅛ teaspoon salt

1¼ cups buttermilk

½ cup sucanat (granulated cane sugar) or raw sugar (available at most health food stores)

¼ cup unsweetened applesauce

1 large egg

2 tablespoons canola oil

1 teaspoon vanilla

Yield: 12 muffins

Preheat the oven to 375 degrees. Lightly grease twelve 3 × 1½-inch muffin cups with pan spray.

In a medium bowl, mix the bran, the flours, baking soda, and salt. Set it aside.

Using an electric mixer, beat the buttermilk, sucanat or sugar, applesauce, egg, oil, and vanilla until frothy. Add the dry ingredients and fold them until they are just combined.

Divide the batter equally among the muffin cups, filling them to the top. Bake the muffins until their tops spring back when pressed gently in the middle, about 30 minutes.

Cool the muffins in the pan for 10 minutes and remove them to a wire rack.

Multigrain Muffins

These muffins are denser, grainier, and a lot healthier than your average muffin. I loved the flavor, but I found them a little dry, so I made them moister by adding applesauce. That did the trick!

Preheat the oven to 400 degrees. Grease nine 3 × 1½-inch muffin cups.

In a large bowl, combine the flours, oatmeal, cornmeal, sugar, baking soda, baking powder, and salt.

In a separate bowl, whisk the buttermilk, oil, molasses, egg, and applesauce together until they are combined. Fold the buttermilk mixture into the dry ingredients. Fold in the raisins, sunflower seeds, and flax seeds.

Spoon the mixture evenly into the prepared muffin cups, filling them to the top.

Bake the muffins for 18 minutes or until a cake tester or toothpick inserted into the center of one muffin comes out clean.

½ cup all-purpose flour

½ cup whole wheat flour

¼ cup buckwheat flour (You can substitute another flour if you don't have buckwheat. Use more all-purpose or whole wheat flour, or try something different, like soy flour or amaranth.)

¼ cup oatmeal, quick or old-fashioned

½ cup cornmeal

2 tablespoons firmly packed dark or light brown sugar

1 teaspoon baking soda

½ teaspoon baking powder

½ teaspoon salt

¾ cup buttermilk

⅓ cup vegetable oil

⅓ cup molasses

1 large egg

½ cup applesauce

½ cup raisins

¼ cup sunflower seeds

¼ cup flax seeds (You can substitute chopped nuts for the seeds if you wish.)

Yield: 9 muffins

Index